Feelings are the pathway to your soul

A selection of teachings from Bob Moore

The Vigilant Self

*My inner world, is one of constant endeavour to remain in
accord with and listen to the Presence
who speaks in the Stillness,
To stay aware of the radiance of light
which illuminates my thoughts
and moves me beyond,
To extend this consciousness outward in silence
and communication in everyday life.*

© 2012 Daniel Perret
Publisher Books on Demand GmbH
12/14 rond point des champs Elysées
75008 Paris, France
Printed by Books on Demand GmbH
Norderstedt, Deutschland
ISBN 9782810623464
Dépôt légal avril 2012

Bob Moore – Feelings are the pathway to your soul

Photo: Bodil Egeberg

Bob Moore – Feelings are the pathway to your soul

This compilation is being published with Anni Moore's consent.

Cover photo: D. Perret
Buddha from Afghanistan, Musée Guimet, Paris

This Buddha statue from 12th century Afghanistan shows the (rim of) mental aura as we know it and as Bob taught it. This particular sculpture represents the 'The Initiation of Fire and Water'

Many people have contributed to this compilation with their work, either of spending hours transcribing Bob's teachings from audio tapes or correcting them. I would like to thank them in the name of all readers of this book. I would also like to thank the people who have helped me by talking over some aspects of this collection and especially Marie Perret for doing the final editing.

Introduction

Bob's teachings are essentially an oral transmission which included numerous exercises, meditations and practices. These are passed on by his students and cannot, in my conviction, be part of this, nor any other book. Oral transmission is by far more precise and complete than any written transmission. This has been proved scientifically ...and through experience. Oral transmission therefore needs a teacher, someone to explain, to show, to answer questions, to give a sense of what is happening while doing exercises and meditations, a sharing in a group where one can also see how rich and manifold the individual experience can be around the same exercise. One needs to have the guidance of a teacher who has practiced them for a long time themselves and therefore can encourage and guide how often they should be done and when.

This present collection mainly includes texts about development and the right attitude to growth of mind and compassion. We have not included exercises, meditations and practices, and have avoided technical descriptions about energy structures (chakras, energy points, energy fields, etc.), nor will you find much about the transpersonal psychology Bob has linked to all these structures. All these aspects are either better taught or, where suitable, published in some books. You'll find a list at the end of this book. You can search for keywords in the index at the end of the book.

We'll include a single exercise as an example at the end, so that the new reader can get a sense of what Bob's exercises were like. The way to do them is explained in detail in 'The Science of Spiritual Healing', which is essentially based on Bob

Moore's teachings. The present texts have been transcribed from audio tapes. They cannot be a substitute to personal discipline and transformation exercises or meditation. They are though a beautiful complement and companion.

The reason for publishing this collection of quotes from Bob Moore comes out of the realisation that as good one's own teaching can be, second generation students of Bob's work will never be able to hear his unique way of explaining the development process, the aim of spiritual growth and his 'philosophy'. Bob had a rare way of expressing himself, very clear, very heartfelt and never just intellectual. We think this comes through in this selection of texts from him. They are beautiful windows into our soul's journey.

Although he was deeply connected with the spiritual world, Bob saw it as his task to help us ground spiritual energies. He thus developed a unique way of connecting us to the physical body, to precise parts of it and to exploring the deeper purpose of each energy point, each part of the body. In doing this he managed to make us realise the link between the sub-conscious, the body, our ego and emotions and how to transform these aspects in order to allow our deeper essence to manifest and express.

This collection of texts came about urged by the desire of 'second generation' Bob students to know more about Bob Moore and the felt knowledge he shared with us. This is a selection of talks he gave during courses. We have given the references at the end of this book. These texts have brought us insights and understanding even when reading them, some texts, up to 30 years after they had been given. They are timeless inspirations. They are treasures. May your heart open to let them sink in.

The essence of Bob Moore's teachings may well be expressed in the title of this book: "Feelings are the pathway to your soul." Indeed, when we endeavour to understand the essential part of ourselves and of life, we turn to the spiritual dimension and to how it is felt deep within us. By definition there is nothing to measure, nor to weigh or see with our physical eyes in the spiritual realm. In order to explore it we can only do so through our feelings. Feelings are not just part of the upper astral, or transformed emotions, but extend way beyond this. So that when experiencing the spiritual in search of our soul, our higher self, the deepest or divine part of ourselves, we must rely on our feelings. Once we have transformed our subconscious we get a clearer access to intuition and can more easily discern between genuine feelings and the illusions of the ego. Then we can train ourselves to acquire a precision in observing and expressing feelings.

In reading these teachings one has to be aware that they were given in a specific context: a) of a certain group - see p. 85 - b) of a certain time and c) during a particular phase of Bob's teachings. In the1980's Bob would often talk of developing the pineal, whereas in the 1990's and later he put more emphasis on working with more precise points, such as the reflector point, blend point, above ear points and the centre of the head. Similarly he practically dropped for some years talking about the ID- or Individuality-Point and talked more about the focus position instead, realising probably, that this position was the obstacle to work on if one would want to get a real contact to the ID-Pont.

I know for myself that Bob is still engaged in teaching, even though he is now dwelling in the spiritual dimension. You cannot talk about and believe in the spiritual dimension and imagine that a soul like his just disappears; neither do we when we die. He is still present, so is the depth of feeling in these texts.

Daniel Perret

Let Bob take over now:

It's very difficult to produce descriptions of feeling. Having worked with people for many years now, it seems to me that the word feeling has been strongly related to emotion. One can look at feeling and find that if one follows the movement through emotional conditions within us, one of course is drawn to feeling. One can look at that and say that it is the upper bracket of emotion. It is. But then that doesn't end the connection to feeling. In fact one can say that is only the beginning.

The process of growth is something that never stops. It is always continuing. In this continuity we can find that everything that we work with is a preparation for something else. When we would cease that activity, then we cease the relationship to growth. With this whole perspective in development of healing, you may recall, we worked through different chakras and so brought into being symbols that were showing up through a meditative process with each chakra. **Symbols** we have always viewed as very important, because we find in the use of symbols, we are producing a thought structure. Thought structures of themselves are part of the whole process of energy formation. **Energy always follows thought**.

We don't always find the same structures of thoughts being used. We have got structures of thoughts that of themselves are very much reflecting our ego or emotional attachment to various situations or experiences. Such thought patterns are not registering the deeper aspect related to the product of thought. In the various degrees that we find associated with the different thought patterns, we have different energy structures following the producing of a thought structure. Thought structures of themselves are part of the whole process of thought patterns. This is something that can be viewed in a somewhat different way from what we see working in other degrees or aspects of development. One of our reasons for having separate healing workshops was simply because healing is an increasingly exact science. It is no longer something that one could find many years ago, when people used their hands without structures of knowledge.

Healing is becoming more and more an activity of understanding that relates to higher degree of energy that is formulated from an initial impulse - and so graduates to thought performance. Thought performance itself then produces action. And so we have this combination of impulse, which perhaps we can look on as the connection between spirit and soul, from that impulse we have the movement of the energy into the brain structure, and from there that movement into the physical activity and hence outward into an expression beyond the physical.

In this healing we have endeavored to divide it into two categories: one, that is loosely called "self healing". Second the expression of higher consciousness of energy towards other people in the use of hands or aura structures. Both of these aspects are very much related, self healing is to me something tremendously important. Certainly as far as I am concerned, I would not be here now, unless I had been brought to an under-standing of what self healing really is. This aspect of working on oneself is to me a basic aspect of understanding the whole purpose of unifying different levels of consciousness so as to create a balanced expression outward.

Within this process that we have been working through, we have been using as well as symbols, **colours.** We have also been using sound. We have come to understand colours in different ways. Not just the colour itself, but the vibration which is the construction of the colour. Although we may not see colour, everyone has the means of sensing the vibration, which is the colour. Therefore colour plays a big part within the whole structure of healing.

When we come to **sound,** we have used various types of sound, various pieces of music. And so we have learned to define some sounds, as we find them reflected into the aura structure or penetrating another person's aura structure. Sound itself is also vibration and so related to the colour vibration. So we get this combination which many people are working with throughout the world at the present time.

We have worked through the physical body through different systems in the body. As for example, we have worked with the polarity system, the lymph system, the nervous system. We have linked up these three systems with the flow of energy that we see operating with each person etherically. The energy that we have called the eight streams in the body. And when I say body, I am speaking about the combination of etheric and physical. These energy streams in the body, many people have incorporated them in their work now, with other people.

This relationship between the etheric and the physical forms a basis of understanding of the flow, the movement of energy from other bodies of expression within each individual, as for example the mind body. The different movements of energy that we see in each chakra have their connection with different levels of contact, that each of us can use or work with, so that each of the chakras not only form their own pattern of vibration but also produce their own effect through the connection they have with the different bodies of expression. They produce their own effect between the etheric and the physical.

When we come to structures that we find in the subtle anatomy of an individual, we have - if we look at it energy wise - somewhat of a similar connection to the anatomy structures of the physical body. When we look at other bodies, embodied in this physical that we have, we find structures of energy which are moving in patterns and moving in rhythms. Patterns and rhythms are what we see of energy that makes up that particular body, such as the mind body. We have been trying to have people get a deeper appreciation of the relationship of energy and body performance. In the prana science course, we have reached the point to move into a chakra to experience the inward draw and the outward movement that can be experienced with each chakra, (...to have the awareness inside the chakra itself). These movements of energy that we find in chakras are important when we come to try to understand what we are using in a healing process either with ourselves or someone else.

Vibration, one of the structures of all the ethers that we find around us, vibration that has four movements (four layers, DP) in the ether that is in this room, this vibration is what we draw on when we work in a process of healing on another person. Each of the chakras responds to these states of vibration. The sensing of the movement of energy that we experience with the use of our hands are also related to changing vibration.

When we originally used the symbols we worked with in each of the chakras, we were using those symbols first of all in relation-ship to the balance of prana, **prana** meaning life force. Balance of prana is one of the essential aspects in the movement of energy outward. The balance of prana is very much involved with the **spleen**. The spleen is not a development chakra. It is a chakra whose responsibility is to distribute prana to some other chakras. This distribution of prana also involves a cleansing process just as the physical spleen is involved in that type of process. We find that the relationship to especially four chakras: root, solar plexus, heart and thyroid, is very important, when we look at emotions.

Again distinguishing emotions from **feelings**, **emotions** are the uncontrolled connection with higher consciousness. I am saying uncontrolled although emotions are extremely important. When we do not have the means of controlling the thought involvement related to emotional extension then we have an unbalanced situation in the chakras beneath the thyroid. That unbalanced situation does not allow the spleen to distribute prana energy as it needs to distribute it. And so we find in such an unbalanced situation, that this is requiring a lot of our energy attention. This means we have less energy to be used in a giving situation, because emotions of this type are always a holding or introvert aspect. And healing can never be introvert, even a self healing process. It has got to use the same process of energy that we see working in all life: contraction and expansion as a simultaneous activity.

When we come to thought in relationship to symbols: The structure of symbols is something that we of ourselves can induce or it is something that can be brought to us by the function of energy or a thought structure that is moving too quickly for us to assimilate. These symbols, that we have been using, are based on the three aspects that we see functioning most predominantly with all energy: **circle, square** and a **triangle**. Each of those symbols reflects the movement of energy that of itself blends different vibrations together and from that blend produces effect.

To formulate these symbols with our thoughts, is to produce, in whatever area of consciousness we are using at that particular time, a movement of energy which allows the thoughts to construct something that we can view as positive. I am using this term 'positive' in this sense at this time, although it is not in the processes of healing a reality. We use terms as 'negative' and 'positive', but the reality of healing is that it is neither negative nor positive. The reality of healing is neutral. We are using these terms purely as descriptive terms between two aspects.

But always in healing we have the third aspect brought in and that third aspect means a change or a rise of consciousness. We can see this in one of the symbols: the **triangle**. We have the base line. It represents the two aspects. One we can view as negative the other we can view as positive. We could say in this triangle we have a positive and a negative pole. The negative and positive pole of energy movement are related purely to the polarity that shows up with each of us, until we reach a certain point.

On our original chart right in the beginning ... it showed the polarity structure up to the meditation line. When we move through the meditation line, we come to the Buddhic or soul area. Within those five senses that related to the soul area, we are beyond polarity. We are not structuring in negative or positive. Within that Buddhic or soul area is the only place, the only part where we mention healing. Negative or positive therefore relates to the flow of energy that we see as a necessity to structure things that are related to physical growth or physical conception. This negative and positive is what we use to bring the two poles together. But when we bring the two poles together, when we have a balance in that, we create. That creation is of itself not negative or positive. It is creation of joining, where the negative and positive have become one, within another state of consciousness. It is in that other state of consciousness where we have the blend between - what I am calling - spirit and soul. That would be represented in the triangle in the upper point, being the neutral point.

That neutral point is very significant in the whole processes of healing, because if we really are going to be functioning with ourselves or towards other people, then we have got to disassociate ourselves with like or dislike, the negative and positive aspect. We have got to be used to be a vehicle of expression in giving or allowing that energy to function with the higher aspect of thought. This does not mean at all, that we just become robots to something that we don't understand. It means, that we are learning to appreciate that we have a contact with a dimension of consciousness that allows a flow of energy to function without our physical limitations. We limit ourselves completely when we bring ourselves into the sense of liking and disliking another person.

This triangle therefore represents the means of allowing the influence of a higher consciousness to function into a physical plane of expression. You may recall: this triangle forms part of the symbol that we had related to the heart. The other part of the symbol was a circle. The circle making contact with the triangle in each of the three points. We used this symbol on the heart because the triangle is representing balance, which is absolutely necessary to have in the whole performance of healing. The circle represents continuity, the flow of energy which has no beginning and no end. It is a flow that operates because the contact has been achieved with the area that really matters. This is one of the chakras we are going to be working with predominantly this week.

The other chakra we are going to be working with during this week is the thyroid. The **thyroid**, again, is one of the most important chakras that we have. The channeling of energy in transmutation from the bottom of the body towards the pineal or crown, can only function through the balance of the thyroid. The thyroid chakra is a chakra of sound. That sound is related to the various aspects of expression that we use in different forms of healing. It also is a chakra which shows release.

When I am speaking about **release**, I am not just speaking about emotional release. I am speaking about the whole release of energy that shows up in these different levels around the physical body within the aura structure. That release is a movement. The thyroid is a chakra very strongly related to karmic situations. Karmic structures as part of the past life sequence of activity are also reflecting states that we see preventing the thyroid operating correctly.

Often we can find with people this **karmic** structure situation linking up with **hereditary factors** and so producing strong emotional situations which produce a repressive situation within the person, which then prevents the thyroid from functioning as it needs to function. The thyroid accepts the energy that moves upwards from the other chakras towards the pineal. If it of itself is not in a balance, that movement of energy upwards does not reach its contact with the pineal.

It is necessary to allow the pineal to have the correct balance of energy from the lower chakras if that pineal is to operate in an intuitive sensing, or as we called it in the original chart 'higher clairvoyance'. Healing is not concerned with astral clairvoyance. ...

You must remember that **the thyroid** first and foremost is a chakra of expression. I don't just mean the use of voice. When there is interference in that expression, the interference will show up predominantly on each side rather than in the center of the thyroid chakra. The center is, as it were, the combination of interference, or the release of interference that allows this energy in the center to be very hard or in a much softer aspect. ...

We have nine secondary chakras in the chest area and we have got two on the pubic bone. The two on the pubic bone have a tremendous significance related to sensitivity. There is so much related to the anatomy structure of the physical body and the subtle anatomy structure outside the physical body and sensitivity, that when we come to (restrictive) movements of energy (e.g. between the sec. chakras on pubic bone and thyroid) The thyroid itself is always responsive to blockages or difficulties even from other chakras, that may be in an unbalance. ...

Movement of the physical body (while doing exercises, DP) is often an escape when you do exercises like that. If you just move your head, you change your contact with yourself in what you are doing. If you are structuring something that represents balance, if you are getting an effect on the body, try to keep the body in the same position. ... Once you move your body in relationship to changing thought patterns, then you disturb all the thought structures that you are trying to produce around you. If you are drawn to your body, keep moving out again. It can be quite rewarding to keep moving out, in such a situation, this could help a change in something that may be held or trapped in the way of energy on the etheric. If you move your body you cannot create that change. ... What may be coming through the body may be energy related to the blockage (in moving the body), but it is not helping to clear the blockage. The energy might not be coming from the quality area. You can use your body in movement *after* an exercise.

These **symbols** we are working with, they represent something that is showing up on different levels. The other dimensions, which lie beyond the connection between, say the physical, etheric and astral. The other dimensions are also functioning. But they may not be functioning in the same directive or with the same directive that you have used physically. So, when we come to movement - and this is something that is difficult to explain, you can only experience it - that we are defining as physical movements or that have been structured with our physical thoughts, often that movement is going in the reverse.

This is because energy activity is not of itself controlled by our physical concepts.

Changes do not occur like magic in healing

When we come to the **changes** that are reflected in the things that we are doing, those changes are often happening on a deeper dimension before they show up on the physical. Many times I have had people saying to me: 'I have been doing those exercises from the last course for three months and I don't find any changes happening to me physically. I feel sometimes there is something, but I don't know what it is.' After a little time the same person comes again and says: 'I no longer do that thing that I did physically, or I no longer express myself the same way physically. It just happened over night'. But of course it did not happen over night. It happens over a period of time, because the exercise was working in a deeper dimension. Gradually it has brought this change about in the other dimensions before it is reflected into the physical. This is something really worthwhile thinking about, especially related to healing.

Changes do not occur like magic in healing. They build up over a period of time. It is just the same: your physical structure was not the first thing that was formed with you. Your etheric structure was already in existence before your physical was structured. The reality is, it is not the etheric that is a counterpart of the physical, but the physical is a counterpart of the etheric. ...

If we can just learn to trust that higher consciousness works even though it doesn't work like magic, but it works, if you continue to do these (exercises) all the (interferences) ... will gradually be changing. The changes that come about, you would see in your everyday attitude towards things or how you would be looking at things.

... The person's own healing capabilities are the strongest thing within any individual. They are stronger than another person's healing towards that individual. That healing capability of the person themselves links to their own qualities. This quality relationship is essential to the natural movement of energy. (Giving healing) …towards another person helps them in the atunement from your qualities to the other person's qualities. That is helping the qualities of the other person to move into the denser areas of the aura, and then it is first of all the quality energy that makes contact with the natural movement of energy with the other person. The natural movement of energy then begins its own process of gaining strength to make a difference or a change in the blockage of energy or the emotional situation.

When we come to **apparent instantaneous healing**, there is no such a thing. There is no magic in healing. Instantaneous healing is something that has been worked for, for a long time. And it has often come about because of struggling, illness, sorrow all having been gone through and so allowing the person to reach a point where they can blend with a higher energy. And that removes the restriction. Although illness is something none of us want, but illness also has its positive aspects. ... (If that person) has really understood, what has caused their illness or what is behind their illness, then that person is being made ready to receive healing. And with the combination from a person who is working from their quality area towards that person who is ill, then there is a fusion of spiritual energy. That fusion then penetrates the denser areas. So a change takes place.

All these aspects of healing are very much related to spirituality, higher consciousness, trust, faith, compassion. But equally it is scientific in what we find related to energy. And I am quite sure, that one of the things that is going to be showing as important in the time ahead is what we can find healing doing in **combining science with religion**. Because we have this combination, and it is really a unique combination when we start to get the understanding of it, that **faith** is not a blind faith. It combines with knowledge, and that knowledge leads to wisdom. Working within the aura structure is very valuable knowledge, but it is not the beginning and the end of everything. It leads us to a faith, to appreciating that we can see so far, but then as we are moved into more depth of awareness, then something else takes over. And so I am sure as we advance in knowledge, get deeper in to the understanding of energy flow and energy movement, then the increase of our faith brings more things about. ...

———

We can work through all these exercises and you can experience all these things in the group. But you have got to look for, what you experience in **your normal everyday life** as a change. That is the test of anything that you do in a group. You have got to look, giving it a little bit of time, for something changing in your everyday attitude in your everyday life.

Many people can have **fear** - and the fear of course is attached to the solar plexus - but often one of the reason the fear is there, is because the person has been rejected. If you are rejected it is a hurt situation, it is a heart situation. If you have broken through that, that gives you the means of overcoming that element of fear related to the rejection. So this is where you get a combination between the solar plexus and the heart. That is why **exercises** like this are so important to work with. Because you are not doing something to force any release. It is coming in a natural way because you have reached the point, where you are recognizing something in an area of consciousness that allows a different movement to take place. And that becomes a permanent change.

—

Meditation itself is a very precise way of working with yourself in drawing in cosmic energy. The precision in meditation can really only be understood when you have started to - as it were - make some physical sacrifice in what you are doing. I am using this term of physical sacrifice because the discipline aspect in meditation is extremely important. In the quietness achieved in meditation, we need to have control over our thoughts. This is where there are many difficulties.

Because if we start out, e.g. to go through one of these questions (your motives and where they come from, concerning healing), perhaps some of you have found, perhaps for a couple of minutes you are going through some process related to the question and suddenly your thoughts are going somewhere else, or other thoughts are coming in. The reason that happens is because the thought process that you have started out to use with the question, relates to a dimension in which you want to get more understanding. But after a little time other dimensions come in with your thoughts. And so the dimension you begun with is disrupted.

The aspect related to meditation is **control** and this control relates to thought. One of the best ways one can begin to have the correct contact with meditation is by getting the body in a set and relaxed position. So that your body does not **move** during the period you are doing meditation. This is something that is pretty important in centering. If you are going to try and center yourself before you work with another person, you will not be able to center yourself if your body is moving, because you are destroying the aspect of your thoughts that is endeavoring to bring you in contact with higher consciousness.

In the aspect of moving when you work on another person, this movement has to be under some... (control, DP). When you realize that your hands have a strong contact with your heart - the area of the heart relating to the sense of touch - then this movement of your hands related to energy is also very much related to centering or how you have centered yourself.

———

When we come to use energy between ourselves and another person our aura structure is very much involved with that, not just our hands. Our thoughts are very much involved with that. So the quality part of the aura is very much connected with circulation, when we use this symbol, or combine this symbol in this way, we are combining not only the heart connection as a heart connection, also the attitude, or as we had in the meditation this morning our beliefs or our needs. All of that is involved between ourselves and another person. This is what makes healing such a precise aspect. Everything that we do is involved with healing: our own personal lives, every bit is as much connected with healing, as when we stand in front of the person to place our hands on them. The whole process of energy movement is something that happens with us in all situations that we are involved with.

———

Although the **hands** are not the only thing we use in healing - we are also using the aura structure, and of course the energy of the solar plexus and the heart. But hands represent so much in the movement of energy and direction of energy. When you consider how much our thoughts link to our hands each day, then perhaps you can see that we have a very strong connection between the area of control and the action of the hands.

If we can bring this to a deeper or higher dimension, then the activity of the hands responds to that area of control. The response in it shows up perhaps more strong than it does in other contexts or with other parts of the aura, because we have a very strong physical thought movement to the hands. So we have something we can direct a thought image towards. This makes a lot of difference, because then it gives us an objective point through which we can produce a realistic... (effect? DP)

All healing is a realization. The realization may not be accomplishing miracles over night. But like so many realizations that we have in life, they build up slowly. This is what is happening in healing. It is a change that is happening slowly. The·change of itself is not just the energy from one person changing the energy of another person. The change comes about when there is a blend between two people, that allows the person who is obtaining the healing to get more under-standing of themselves and their own process and why they contacted the illness to begin with. That is also important in working things through or understanding our pathway or our role in life.

When we come to use our hands, areas that we find in the body can be used to help us build up the energy strength through our hands. Over two years ago, we had an exercise where we were using our breathing from the heat point up and down each arm into each hand. We used that exercise then to try to bring the awareness of what can happen in this heat point related to transmutation of energy.

——

Intuition is the controlling influence that dictates to us when we work with another person. So the whole relationship between meditation as a centering and the movement that we use in working with another person has its relationship in its contact with intuition or spirituality. This is important in so far as healing is concerned, that I would place on the meditative process.

——

Physical security is one of the most damaging things that we have, because that itself is a separation from higher conscious- ness which involves fear. The reality is you do not need physical security. Physical security will always come if you have placed your trust or you energy into higher consciousness. There will never be a problem with physical security. But when we hold on to physical aspects, then we separate ourselves from higher consciousness. So it is not possible then to have physical security. Physical security is not based on the values of material essence. Money for example, is not related to physical security. Money is an energy that is used as a controlling influence, which of course many people misuse. So it brings it into another definition. But the reality of money is that it is an energy that circulates. And money itself relates to higher consciousness when we come to understand what higher consciousness is in relationship to security.

The heart chakra is the fourth chakra upward. It is the chakra that takes us beyond the personality level if we allow it to operate. Or if it is not functioning correctly, then it embodies all the aspects of the personality which assume a very hard energy. The hard energy then is the analytical energy, the energy that wants all sorts of things for itself. It is the ego aspect coming into prominence.

When we look at the whole process of the difference of ego as distinct from the 'I', we have such a vast difference. Many people have great difficulty in separating ego from 'I'. If you are involved with ego then often so much of what you are doing you may consider to be related to 'I', but in actual fact it is related to ego. The heart chakra represents the chakra that has the means of transmuting or transforming the energy of the lower personality obtained or conditioned by the three movements of energy in the lower chakras. So that if we have this contact with the heart, and that has been progressed through the thyroid to the pineal and crown, then in that process we have the means of transmuting the energy from the lower chakras upwards. So we complete the circulation of energy.

The heart chakra relates to the progress of energy that is taking us to another defined situation within ourselves. These twelve sections when we talk about the heart chakra being open. This does not mean like opening a door. The reality of it is that it is drawing in the various vibrations of energy so that each of the sections contributes to the overall movement of vibration from this chest area of the body. That overall movement, when we are looking for balance between physical and higher consciousness, is the blending of spiritual energy and prana energy. This blend is necessary if we are going to have a balance in any chakra. It is necessary simply because we have a chakra - not a development chakra - the spleen chakra. Its purpose is to distribute prana through a number of the other chakras. One of these chakras is the heart. And so the heart represents the balance that is showing up with the universe, or like energies that we have from the sun ultra violet, infra red, electricity, light and such like.

And the other aspect is the relationship that we have to the **soul**. I am using this term soul, but I don't know what a soul is. I have never seen a soul as far as I know. All I have seen is this individuality point, which some teachers call the soul. I can see the individuality point has its connection with the heart. I am using the term soul simply because to me, there has to be something that shows as an intermediary in a non-physical connection between a spiritual force and a physical expression. That intermediary I am calling the soul.

So, if this heart is to function correctly, then we have to develop the attitude of giving something to other people without looking for a return. That is compassion. That differs greatly from the ego content, which is always looking for a return. The return that is related to higher consciousness is a return, in which there is no preset conditions attached to it. The return is related to what you are finding within your own higher consciousness. ...

When we combine what is happening in the heart ... it brings us to the whole spectrum of color that we have used in this heart chakra. Every chakra has its relationship to the heart. Every aspect of color is related to the heart. The heart shows the difference when we look at the whole combination of color in the heart. (The green of the heart) ... is the only color that is a horizontal color. Every other color related to any other chakra is a vertical color. This means, that the heart has got to have its balance with each other chakra.

So each other chakra is contributing to the movement of energy out from the heart. That movement of energy is what you are finding or contacting when you are working in your own aura structure related to the heart, is a soft movement. So you are getting a big difference between the energy movement from the heart and the energy movement of any other chakra. ...

from "Healing" Course 21.-27.5.1983, transcription D. Perret

———

Joy is the movement of love

that reflects in the inner self

and becomes expressed outwards.

Bob Moore – Feelings are the pathway to your soul

It doesn't matter whether your **belief** relates to Mohamed or to Christ or God or Universal Consciousness or whatever, if that belief has given you the means to open yourself, to be receptive to a higher state of consciousness, then you can use that higher state of consciousness because you have increased the activity of the energy flow through your whole being and that is what shows in your aura structure.. ....of course it is more effective if you have reached a state of your consciousness in which you are not holding on to your blockages or whatever.

How do we separate our wants from our needs? What are our needs? Are we learning from our own lives or are we dictated to by other people? Wisdom and spirituality are necessary to move into higher consciousness – in order to find out what is essential to the 'I' (our higher self). To progress we need to keep our feet on the ground and integrate all levels we know of. We have many experiences that we are not able to talk about. They are our own individual ones. But always paying attention, being mindful, gives us the means to move from an emotional position to discover what it is all about.

By using the exercises ourselves, we see what they create on ourselves – through the help of our feelings. We must examine and confront ourselves, in order to get free from inferiority, to be able to contact wisdom. Try to be freer, and do not to project ourselves on what we want other people to be. Look back and reflect: Why did I become angry? What was I scared of? What was I not getting? It is the exactly the same thing with self-pity, and also the start of depression. We must look at the role we play. Experience what we do, and look at dreams in between the sleep state and wakefulness.

There is this story of the tramp lying on the river bank, and dreaming of the rich lady. He ended up in the river. An illusion leads to more illusions. We have got to step outside of ourselves to get to the 'I'. Many ideas of spirituality are our own illusions. Energy is just a tool used in different ways. Much relates to an individual attitude and what we do with our own lives. Any religious structure can always be progressive, but it is a problem when some people set themselves up as an authority. Each of us is in our own level of consciousness and it varies from person to person. We each create our own problems.

There is a need for change to take place; when there is **fear** in connection with the unknown and people don't have the inclination to go beyond it – then the fear is increasing. The exercises are confronting us when we are scared to take the step. The area of pollution is increasing; it is a combination of what we are creating from the way we bring our thoughts into action.

When they talk of breeding a certain kind of pig to produce lungs, kidneys and hearts: is the motivation for doing that coming from a fear of death? In South Korea they had the means of multiplying the cells of human beings but they did not proceed with that; it is not a condemnation but there is no consideration of the end product 10-20 years ahead. These are experiments of knowledge. Where did the original thought come from - the ego? Or was it prompted from above? We can't answer this. There are areas of mind that we do not know, thought structures in a collective state passed from one consciousness to another. There is a total confusion and sometimes it is not possible to analyse. Wisdom is not acquired through knowledge – but wisdom gives a direction to knowledge, it is a higher aspect of us.

To atheists wisdom is the moral standard of an individual. Atheists have no concept of life after death. Is there anything going on after life? Churches have not changed with the times, and do not give people direction to help them move beyond. People who believe are quite prepared to discuss an after-state of life. Some religions have pitfalls, some more than others. Are we able to move beyond this censorship of judgement?

Individuals must decide for themselves. We can develop ourselves so that we do not just hold on to some beliefs we have from our childhood. Energy is alive. It always moves until we close off and then it fights and produces structures in that area, it has to do something. Working with energy has to be progressive. In meditation, we go into something where there is no experience. When you allow yourself to go into stillness you are part of everything, this becomes nourishment, but we are so used to have experiences.

If we are going to develop we have to allow ourselves to reach beyond and venture into the unknown. Nelson Mandela's speech: "The deepest fear we have is not about being inadequate but a fear of our tremendous spirit and energy." If we have taken a step we don't have to talk about it – we radiate it.

Knowledge is retained in the etheric streams, they are part of memory, and they are a storehouse. Changes are related to memory and when we have to confront things. All the exercises combined with meditation help us to rise above our own inadequate structures. Bob has learned from the processes he has gone through himself. What is logic and what is illogic? It is purposeful to understand this difference in learning about energy.

Wisdom is not logic, wisdom can be preposterous, making no sense – but when we progress further it can make a lot of sense. Truth is one of the most essential factors. No one can say they have the ultimate in love or in truth. But the laws of life such as: the law of truth, the law of attraction, the law of cause and effect, the law of love, they are part of the free movement of energy and we must let them work in our lives.

1999 course: "Knowledge to Wisdom", Notes from a participant

The **qualities** seem to me to depend on the age of the soul, how far a soul has progressed or what it has done in past lives to draw forward these qualities and so this is how I see the qualities, that it relates to past-life structures or what has evolved through past live structures. You can find that one person has just one color, quite a lot of people have two colors, not so often you would see three colors. One can be more dominant but the other also produces its activity so that you can have a person that would be very sympathetic towards another person or other people and then you can have another person who would be sympathetic but also would have wisdom to use with that sympathetic situation, so that would be a combination of two things and this, as I see it, also affects the level of development or the level of energy that can be used from one person to another person in healing.

You have some people with much stronger energy, because they are drawing on such things, say, as a combination of compassion and wisdom, whereas another person, who may have all the compassion in the world, they can use that compassion to good effect but they haven't as yet acquired the quality of wisdom so you would have that difference.

When you are expressing qualities, when you are using them, you are always growing in relationship to your soul and of course that is producing other qualities which are eventually being drawn in. I have never seen in the people I know a change in their quality-aura, which makes me understand that the development of qualities must be a long process, but of course the use of quality is always bound to bring you into contact where you can use more qualities, that to me is the whole process of living. I don't see qualities starting at one end of the spectrum and moving to the other end.

To me another factor is drawn into it, because there is always a connection of any quality to the heart and so that connection to the heart seems to suggest to me that the soul needs to express through the heart in order to gain the experience back to itself for it to continue growing. As it is growing, then it is bringing more of itself into qualities to be expressed. I don't see that it is a sort of a pattern moving from one color to another color or one vibration to another vibration like that.

To me there is a center theme in it all which must have some connection to expression from the heart, even though the heart with some people may not be open, but yet there is a heart contact with qualities when a quality is drawn in to be used. There you can always see the connection with the heart. So, I find it difficult to believe that you start off with the red ray and move through the whole spectrum of the seven rays to reach the violet ray, to me that does not make sense from what I can see.

... It does provide a lot of information. That information, if it is real is not always information that we like, but it is information that relates to our purpose and sometimes that means that the purpose, in taking this priority, then means that you have got to look at states that we get into or processes that are there, such as loneliness. Often loneliness is looked on as an emotional situation, but sometimes, if we look at it in a correct way, we could bring it into aloneness, which is something different. Aloneness is often necessary if one is to do something with qualities that is related to purpose. I realize that in situations of working with energy it is not always easy, especially related to personal life structure, but again we have got to look where the priorities are and how those priorities relate to what we really feel we should be doing with our lives.

Qualities of course are quite important in the whole process of healing, qualities such as **"patience"**. Patience is one of the priorities in healing but it is also of course one of the things that is quite necessary if you are trying to work through some problems with another person. Linked with that, you have the other aspect of **"discipline"** or **"responsibility"**. These two are also aspects related to healing and related to what you are doing in your everyday life. Responsibility linking to decisions that you have made and so following those decisions through or carrying them out to a point where perhaps it is not possible to go any further, at least you have used your responsibility insofar as it is possible to use it.

These structures are all related to the flow and the movement of energy between one person and another person, so that when we look at this relationship to energy we are looking at the whole *space* situation. I am using the word space, because if we consider when we are talking about being in our own space or someone else being in their space, if we consider what that means, that each of us occupy a space, that space is ours, it can be affected by people in other spaces, but nevertheless it is our space and it is our responsibility to look after that space. The space is not just what we find in the physical body itself, but in working with aura-structure or energy we know very well that this space can extend outward and so part of the problem between people is that people in one space adversely affect people in another space by their own ego, by what they want from the other person or what they are trying to do to override another person or possess another person.

This means that the space that you are occupying then and extending that out through your own energy then affects the other person in a wrong way. Of course the whole concept of space, insofar as energy is concerned, must also take into consideration the space that exists between one person and another person. What there is between us, what there is between you and I at this very moment, that is as important as the space you are occupying sitting in your chair or I am occupying standing here, because this space between us is full of information.

You are listening to my voice now and so my voice is occupying a space between you and I and as you link into something that has a meaning for you so the words then become transformed into something else, so it is no longer the words that you listen to but what is behind the words and of course this is related to sensitivity. Our sensitivity plays a vital part in the whole role of communication, whether we are honest in what we are saying or not. If we are not honest then of course we are again only using the surface area of ourselves, so **honesty** therefore becomes quite an important factor in the whole structure of using energy.

The quality area is the area that not so many people really have a contact with in working with other people and the reason is that we are all so set on dealing with **problems**. We are all looking for problems and problems form somewhere about 75% of the whole activity of one person to another person. If we are going to get away from that limitation then we have got to develop ourselves more to appreciate the qualities in the other person and that requires doing something different in relationship to the subtle anatomy so we have a means of finding that person's qualities and in finding them allowing those qualities to be used in aiding that person to get a better understanding of themselves and of course that is done through the use of the person's thoughts. So we are back to thought and how we use our thoughts in relationship to our everyday activity or in our relationship to other people.

We can look on healing as an activity to help other people, who have illness or problems. But that is only ONE aspect of healing. The whole area now of expansion in healing is related to what has been called the holistic aspect, which is not just related to the physical, but relating also to the mental, the thought and to the spiritual aspect. And so this holistic aspect of healing then is taking into consideration the whole person and as such then the person who is working with healing - and I am defining healing now as **spiritual healing** - the person who is working with such structures then is working in such a way, or should be, so that what they are drawing into the person they are working with is related to that person's qualities. That may make a difference in the approach that we see in these aspects of healing as distinct from some other processes that are used, but also come under the heading of healing.

Because in all the things that I have seen in the years that I have been working with people the reality of any cure has always been related to a change in the person, a **change of attitude** and that change of attitude then becomes one of the predominant factors in what happens to that person after the healing has taken place.

There is no point in working, as I see it, with a person to produce a temporary change. If in a few weeks or a few months that person is going to regress back to the problem that is not healing. If healing is to be real then that reality has got to function through the various levels of the subtle anatomy, which allow a harmonious state to become part of the whole changing structure. And so, within this then, the things that each of us do are very much related to knowledge, knowledge that we can learn about the physical body, but also feeling, feeling that is related to how we apply that knowledge in its relationship to subtle anatomy, to higher consciousness, to spirituality and so this is the combination then, the combination that I see as important when we come to the whole process of helping another person to find a level within themselves that relates to the level that we have gained in our process as individuals.

.....When we speak about working with an individual and accepting that individual as a whole individual, not just the illness or the problems that we see, then we come to an area that I am calling an area of energy, which to me is a governing factor with each of us and that is the area of quality. I have called it quality simply because when that area is being used then what happens through that individual is different from what it is when the area is not being used and this to me is one of the essential differences from ego as distinct from spirituality.

I am using the word "**spirituality**" because I can't find another word that relates to qualities better than that one. This use of qualities then is a use which must be worked with, build up, understood and, above all, accepted.

I hear so often that people have been working through so many deep problems connected with their parents, things that have been problems through their lives, but then, when I come to talk to those people and when I look at the position of their qualities then I say to myself that they still have quite a way to go because they are working from the same level that you are placing your parents in.

Until that person brings their own qualities into what they are doing with their own work-through, they are not really going to get what they need to get as a release or a clearance. If we look at it from that point of view, then we find that we have different levels of consciousness to work with and so of course then we are left with questions: what are these different levels of consciousness? Why should they be there? What is their purpose?

So again, when we go to the aura-structure, which is so much a mine of information, if we could just spend a little more time trying to develop the psychic, which is really the area between qualities and the physical, so that we could come to a realization of energy around a person, then we would see more clearly what we are talking about in the whole structure of working through things, in the whole structure related to physical consciousness as distinct from other areas of consciousness. This you can see in the aura structure, we often hear about, the **health aura**. Consider, what is the health aura? In what area of consciousness does that reside?

If we have a part of the aura-structure that is showing the physical and mental health, then that area of consciousness is an area that is doing something in the aspect of control or otherwise of the physical mechanism. But what is beyond that to create the effect that is being shown in the health aura? It is an area beyond that we are trying to get a better established contact with, that is what healing is all about, that is the depth or the height of healing.

Healing does produce change. If it is properly applied it will produce a change in everyone no matter who that person is, because none of us is perfect, and so healing, applied correctly from the level of quality, will always be helpful to another person, irrespective of illness or no illness. To apply healing properly means that we have got to have this contact with our qualities and to have a contact with our qualities means working on ourselves, but not working from this area of trying to be perfect in the sense of trying to eliminate our problems, but trying to work in the sense that we have something because of how our qualities are structured to share or to give to other people. There is so much involved with this, so much related to a movement of energy which has yet to be learned. I am just talking about the area that I have seen changing with people when they have come to get more or a deeper understanding of a healing process. When some people want a particular term placed on healing, they may be limiting what they require, but nevertheless they have set for themselves some standard that they realize they think is necessary.

When we come to health there must be standards that we set for ourselves, standards that are not just related to what we do when we are working with a person but standards that we have in our everyday lives. We can't just switch standards in our lives from one position to another position. Standards are something that we have as a base upon which we grow and that involves us in everything that we are doing. This energy of quality is an energy that is always showing, exemplifying what we have on a deeper level to express or to share or to give.

I know that many people want to get the realization of all that they call the scientific aspects related to healing and I don't see anything wrong in that, but one thing I have realized: the more we learn the more we realize how much there is still to learn and this shows up when we come to energy itself and how energy works in our own physical mechanism, how we apply our thoughts to ourselves even apart from how we apply our thoughts to other people, thoughts being the wave-length that carries energy. That is something really to think about.

We have to get an understanding that we are not a physical body with a soul, but rather that we are a soul with a physical body. That is rather worthwhile thinking about, because this area of higher consciousness already exists before you are physical, it is existing in movement out of the physical body, it is existing when you no longer have a physical body. I have tried to analyze the death process from my own experience of leaving my body and from watching people die. In that process I can see that the whole physical level of structure, related to the earth elements, plays a part when you will die, it plays a part simply because in each of the four earth elements there is energy, energy that is moving you into different degrees or dimensions within yourself and so the earth is playing its part and the structure of the earth is playing its part in freeing you from gravity.

And when you are no longer in your physical body, then gravity no longer plays a part in your contact with the earth. You are in a completely different dimension, but the one thing that is very strong in that dimension is your thoughts, how you think and how you have developed your thoughts in relation-ship to your higher consciousness - I am calling it **higher consciousness** simply because it is then divorced from the physical structures you are so used to each day. In that state then your thoughts become a predominant part in your whole activity of movement or expression. It is exactly the same if we transfer that situation to the physical. Your thoughts are determining so much about your physical activity, the use of your physical body and furthermore, the use of the energy that surrounds the physical body.

That brings me to the use of colors and symbols. This came to me over 20 years ago related to meditation. Meditation for me became something very valuable, valuable because I was excited about it, excited because I found in meditation I was going into some states I didn't know existed. In those states I found that various things were coming forward such as these exercises and then gradually I had the insight that they could be applied to the physical and the non-physical levels of our make up. I realized that they could be used to make change that can allow a person to establish a better contact with their qualities and so I began using some of those things.

It is easier to get a connection with a person's qualities on the left side. That is one of the reasons why we used the left shoulder. Although we can have on the left shoulder-point as on the right shoulder point a lot of connection from emotional structure in the aura interfering into the mental aura, but on the left side we have more definite movement which is drawn inward to the heart from the quality area which makes a difference in the left shoulder point from the right shoulder point. Of course this is not always felt like that because if a person has got a lot of emotions or depression or such like then both points are affected. This tends to cover up the quicker movement of energy and of course the person may also have a resistance, if they have strong emotions or depression, then their attitude is not open to qualities and so they have a feeling of being very emotional through jealousy or anger or whatever. Alternatively in depressive states a person may feel hopeless and then of course they have closed themselves off to the draw-in of qualities or they are closing themselves off from the vitality of the life force, but that position (around the left shoulder point) would be a good position to try to look for the qualities, between there and the ID-point.

…..if healing is going to be working correctly then we are always looking for the cause or to change what has created that illness. If we are going to do that, then we have to be in contact with a level of energy or if you like, an intelligence that can eradicate the cause. That intelligence has given us, as I see it, our qualities or we have grown with our qualities to reach towards the intelligence and so if we are going to channel towards another person, then the relationship from our qualities to contact the person's qualities, who is in need, that to me becomes a very important aspect of the healing. Because that blend then is bringing in that strength of energy which can be transformed from that level down through the different levels to that person's physical body and in this way then the person, who is receiving the healing is being uplifted to a different attitude.

I have never seen a person who has been cured through healing who have not **changed their attitude to life.** They have always done that and that is simply, as I see it, because the healing aspect has given them something new to understand within themselves, which they may not fully understand, but they are open, which they were not before, and it is the qualities that is a channel for this and of course again what may lie beyond the qualities. That would be the essential thing in healing.

Many people have no idea what their qualities are. You as the healer have a means of contacting your qualities and in that way the contact you achieve with your qualities can bring you into contact with the other person's qualities and it is that blend between your qualities and the other person's that is the important thing. If that is happening then with the quicker movement of energy being brought into the other person, which moves from their quality area into the physical and so that produces an upliftment or a feeling of well-being. It is this feeling of well being that you want to become a lasting feeling and this gives the person more optimism for the future or for whatever they need it.

It is not really necessary for the person to know their qualities but it is necessary in my opinion for that person to want healing. That is the halfway mark, that that person WANTS healing, that they are not being forced by someone else saying: you ought to get something done about this, you go and try this healer. The person themselves must know that they need it, they must want that and once they have achieved that in themselves then that is the halfway mark between you and that person. .....

Each of us has a natural means of using vibration. Each of us has a natural ability to link to vibration to determine differences in vibrations. Of course when we come to apply that with physical consciousness, then we tend to get into all sorts of confusion and problems and we do that simply because we create difficulties for ourselves by the way we live or by the attitude that we have to life.

The whole work with energy is natural. The areas that we see outside the physical body preceded the physical body and it is these areas that show their strong relationship to vibration as it moves through different dimensions to reach the physical. It is here where we create difficulties and this is showing in what we want as physical people instead of what we need. This is for many people a fact, the difference between **want and need**. That fight is not just in the area of emotion itself, it is also in the area of expression or sensing. Sensing and healing very much go together. They are separate, yet they are interrelated and if we can sense more accurately, if we can use knowledge more objectively, then the healing process, which is part of our own qualities, functions with less restriction.

In this whole process of using energy we have always got to try to be ourselves, not try to imitate another person, not try to use something that we have not the ability to use. That makes each of us as individuals unique. There are not two people who have the means of healing in a similar way and the reason is because you are showing differences in what you have as a means of using energy to be worked with in healing. Your qualities are different and so, what each person needs to do in relationship to healing is to try to reach the highest position that your own qualities allow you to reach.

When we talk about qualities we are talking about the contact that we have, as I see it, with the Individuality-point.

So, the qualities that we are using are what we see around each individual, showing up in the different colors or in the different blend of colors. If for example you have a color - let us say blue - in your qualities, you can never make that blue violet or green or yellow. It is blue and that is a vibration that you have got to learn to attune to, to use with another person. I have never seen a person's qualities change - that doesn't mean that there isn't a means to make them change, there may be, I don't know and I haven't seen it. Therefore, if I talk to you about the use of your qualities I am talking to you about the atunement to what the qualities mean for you as an individual.

For example I have mentioned **blue**. Blue is a color of intuition, intuition related to higher consciousness, a source level beyond your emotions. It is a color of tremendous strength. It is a color that helps you to reach beyond your emotions. It is a color that has within it devotion. If you are attuning to blue these things that I have mentioned become part of your qualities that you can use with another person.

That would be different from someone who had **violet** in their qualities. Violet brings you into a different spectrum of quality or, say, red. Many people don't like red and yet, **red** is one of the strongest colors that we can find in relationship to growth. The qualities of red would be related to leadership, courage, or bringing in a means of unifying people, allowing warmth to operate, which is also a heart connection. This dimension of red can also be something that is quite important in healing.

It is much better that you yourself try to find out or understand what your qualities are, and those will surely show to you in anything you are doing towards another person, in which you are not wanting something from the other person. If you are honestly or sincerely giving or sharing with another person, that will always involve your qualities and that is the essential thing in centering and it is that which links you to your understanding of a source level, whatever you consider that source level to be: Universal Mind, Christ, Buddha, whatever it is, your qualities relate you to that belief in a source level.

So, when we talk about healing related to sensitivity, what you are sensing in another person can never take you away from the use of your qualities, as long as you are keeping that sensing into the perspective that you are gaining knowledge or information about the other person in order to produce deeper and better knowledge. In that way sensing and healing become a combination.

Each of us has a natural means of linking with vibration if we can separate ourselves from our own emotions. That always is the reality, not becoming involved with another person emotionally in the process of healing, being objective, but in being objective learning to use your qualities through compassion or such like. So when we come to the process of sensing, objectivity becomes quite important.

Some people have one quality color and other people may have two or three and as far as I can understand it, this seems to me to depend - and here I have to use a term that may not be acceptable to everyone, but it is the only way that I can explain it - on the age of the soul, how far a soul has progressed or what it has done in past lives to draw forward these qualities. I see the qualities as relating to past life structures or what has evolved through past life structures, so one person may have just one color, quite a lot of people have two colors, not so often you see three colors. One can be more dominant but the other also produces its activity as well.

———

The reality of the whole structure of using qualities is to be able to use qualities in a situation that is adverse to qualities being used such as for example in a situation where someone would be angry and this would be an emotional situation. The movement of energy is endeavoring to reach a point of allowing those qualities to be drawn in to an expression even in such situations.

The abilities that you have are the abilities that you were born with. Where these abilities come from, again we can only conjecture about, but there is no doubt that each of us was born with abilities that showed the moment we were born in the aura-structure. A little time ago I watched the birth of a **baby**. When that baby was born, I could see the abilities that that baby has in the aura. Now these abilities will not change.

The color or colors that we see associated with such abilities become more refined, more pastel in their reflection, but those colors themselves will remain throughout that baby's life. Within these colors there is the means of that baby using its energy associated with the abilities or its qualities, with itself and with other people. The things that may prevent that baby from using those abilities could be the mother and father trying to persuade that baby to do something which they feel, of course, is for the baby's good, or it could be the atmosphere or the situation or the emotional content that that baby gets involved with in it's physical life, which will draw that baby in other directions from the use of its abilities.

Now, this being drawn in other directions is something that happens to the majority of people. Since it does happen to most people, then the abilities are often not used. The qualities that you have as an individual can thus be undiscovered. For many people within this whole process of working or functioning in their everyday life, does not allow that individual to give in their expression what they deeply need to give. It is within all of this area that we are endeavoring to get people to appreciate the abilities they have, how to use those abilities and at the same time give them a means to overcome the things that prevent them from using those abilities.

Many people don't believe in reincarnation or don't accept what reincarnation is, but as far as I can see, these states here in the aura, the abilities, have got to come about from somewhere, something has got to produce those. The way I look at it, these abilities have been produced through different life periods of an individual, so that the energy which is built up here within the individual has grown through perhaps many lifetimes.

When we look at the process of an individual in the aura structure that we see around the individual, we look at the area around the physical body which is strongly associated with the etheric. This we call the **health aura,** where illness in the physical body can be seen. When we move beyond that we come into other states of the aura where we can find the astral area of the aura which is where the emotional states show up quite strongly. And then we come to this part where we have the mental area.

When we move beyond that then we come to the soul area and where we have the super conscious area, the spiritual area within that we are moving right outside this structure (of etheric, astral, mental) so we have out here a structure of energy, which we see in color, with some people very refined color. This is the color that we see at birth. When we see the aura at birth, often we don't see the other structures, only these colors and that is your abilities that you can develop, that you can use towards other people.

Those abilities are yours separate from anyone else's. Within those abilities you have the contact with the real part of yourself. The real part of you is not of itself centered in your physical body and yet is part of your physical structure. It is necessary for those abilities or those qualities to operate within your expression. That is why expression is so important.

Often, in order to make contact with your abilities, you have to be working with the inner area of the aura to overcome or release the type of blockage you have. It is important to transform blockages, such as fear, so that they do not drag you to do something or to express in a wrong way, for example: expressing with anger. What we were born with is what we have, in my opinion, accumulated in past lives. What we have accumulated as quality or ability needs to be used in order to allow us to develop and to grow.

With many people, what we see here in the outer area of the aura has not been used. The colors there are not moving. There is no vibration. This outer area of the aura is what we are trying to get a contact with and to allow that contact to operate more and more, so bringing us into a better understanding of ourselves. When we look at ... the use of energy through the Hara, then when we analyze this, this bottom area of the body is building or drawing energy to itself, so that both male and female in sexual expression build up (tension in) that bottom area of the body. I am separating tension from stress - within that tension-buildup it comes to a point where there is release, which causes orgasm or ejaculation.

Within this of course we can have conception, which is bringing into existence another being. That other being is not physical, it has some connection with something beyond the physical or it is in existence somewhere, somehow before the physical body is born. Otherwise what we see here (the quality-area) could not be in existence itself. This quality- or spiritual area of the aura is not related to the mother - in the one birth that I have seen, the quality-area of the child was completely different from the mother's.

Speaking about this movement of energy, which is connected with expression, of course, brings us into the function of the **physical body** as we know it. That is why, when we look at the endocrine gland-system it shows us the importance of balance, for example again when we look at the bottom area of the body: when the ovum breaks free from the ovary it releases two hormones. They move and link up with other hormones, some of them male hormones in the female body, so that within this we have the blend or the balance between the male and female aspects. ....

Often **guilt**-complexes are associated with what has been given to us as teaching or knowledge by other people. When we start to work with ourselves, everything we are doing has to associate with us, so that we are learning to put trust in ourselves, build up some faith in what we are doing, so we can appreciate the purpose that we have, working with other people or indeed being physically alive at this time. And to be physically alive at this time is certainly something that is very demanding. Whether you accept reincarnation or not, I think it must be pretty clear that there is purpose in being alive at this time.

How many of you have become involved in development - this has not come about by mere chance, it has come about because there is purpose in it. It would certainly seem to me that whatever changes lie ahead, there will be some people who will be needed, who have the ability and can use energy that they were born with to help other people. And more and more this is becoming very clear to us that we are making contact, in no matter what country we come to, with people who have this particular type of energy which can be used in working with other people. But so often these energies are not understood. So that in processes like this, working with exercises as we are doing, this often allows that person to get more discipline in themselves, more contact with this energy. Often we can find people getting very quickly into a process of development that allows them to change and make contact with the qualities and abilities that they were born with. These positive aspects of the auric structure are:

RED: will, courage, power, self-dependant, leadership
ORANGE: balance, harmony, rhythm, beauty
YELLOW: tolerance, patience, logic, precision

GREEN: impartial, adaptable, instinctive, mental power
BLUE: intuition, love, wisdom, perception
PINK: devotion, loyalty, service to others, directness
PURPLE: truth, ritualism, activity, integration, vitality, dignity

Often we dismiss **children**'s activities as being childish, but in reality children have a much stronger contact with energy, with sensitivity, with so many things that are connected with their own abilities and we dismiss them as having no significance or as being just childish play. If we would pay attention to what children are doing, we could learn a lot. All this area of expression of the child is not only important to the child. It is also showing a lot towards that child's abilities to express later in his life. This area of abilities shows immediately when the child is born right around the child's body, it is something they bring with them.

.....We have been talking quite a lot about quality-energy, abilities, and the relationship of those qualities to the essence- or **individuality-point** above the physical head. This brings us to another aspect of ourselves, which takes us from the physical level itself into another area of contact with ourselves. This association with the individuality-point has great importance, not just because it is related to what we can use in energy, but because it has its' connection with something that was existing before we were physically born. As to what that was doing (that point, those qualities) before we were physically born, of course this is a matter of conjecture, but, when you look at a birth, it is quite clear that this individuality-point is already existing. So when we trace its function in the aura, then we can see the connection between that and some areas of the aura that are external to what we normally look for in the mental, astral or etheric phases of the aura. These abilities that we were born with are already connected with something that has been in progress somewhere beyond this physical world.

Often when we look at peoples aura-structures, many people have practically no movement in the causal area of the aura. This brings us to the questions: if a person is not using their abilities what value are they to their own individuality or to their own essence, or, if you like, to their own souls. But when you see a person using their abilities, then there is a completely different situation in the complete aura-structure, because this ability-area is moving, is being drawn on by the individual in their expression. It doesn't mean they have to be doing a whole lot of things like healing or massage or working with other people. Even in a normal, everyday job these abilities can work.

What happens, when the abilities are not used or when the emotions are too strong or the "want"-situation is predomi-nant? That is something that I have thought about quite a lot. The reason I am mentioning it now is because, in having people work with the individuality-point it does produce a difference in their aura-structure. It produces a difference out in the quality-area, but also above the head, just above the crown of the head.

I had the fortune once to spend three months with a yogi, quite an old man. We spend a lot of time discussing different attitudes toward life and he taught me a lot about points in the body. These points where apparently used way back in India, many, many years ago, and these points have their relationship to different influences from outside, that show up an effect in different parts of the body.

During the time I was with him a man came to us who had been to Tibet and he had a theory, that if a man didn't take the opportunity that was presented to him in this life to use their abilities, then the whole influence of energy would be so fused, so as to create a destructive force that would destroy this individuality point or as he liked to call it, the soul, and so the soul would burn out. This to me then was a very strange theory, because having been brought up a Christian and trained to be a priest, I didn't understand those sorts of thoughts then, even though I had given up the whole concept of becoming a priest.

But nonetheless these theories that we three talked about stayed with me and as I began this way of teaching, more and more I began to look at people in their relationship to their use of their abilities and so I was increasingly drawn to the big differences that I can see with people, differences that show up where people really are making contact with the their abilities, allowing them to be expressed, and people not really in contact with their abilities, but using quite a lot of intellect or quite a lot of thought-processes as repressive states.

It was during a period when I was doing quite a lot of mediation, a couple of years ago, that so much of all this connection with the individuality-point came forward and it was then that I was reflected back to the mid-1960ties when I had spent about three years in quite a deep process of meditation where I got these exercises that we are working with now and then I became more and more involved with all of this use of the individuality point and the area of the aura that reflects the abilities.

From that point on I began to have people make contact with their own individuality-point. Some teachers call that point the soul, I don't know whether it is the soul, but I haven't got enough understanding of that so I keep calling it the ID-point and I call it that because it seems to me that, when you start to use your abilities, then you do become more of an individual, then you are using the higher aspect of yourself which will link you perhaps in a deeper way to other people. So that is briefly the background to why I have centered so much in this ID-point.

It seems to me that if the reality of development is going to be established with any one of us, then it is not just for the sake of development. The whole psychic potential that each of us has is a potential that takes us either in a wrong way towards the ego-aspect or allows us to be drawn into a higher aspect which does associate itself with the individuality-point.

If you want to develop, if you want to grow, if you want to do something with your abilities you must find a motive for doing it. That motive is your principle to live by, it can't be anything else. It is that principle that gives you the means of achieving your goal, because you have got something there that you have structured as a decision, and all decisions are so important connected with energy. If you make a decision you accumulate all the energy of yourself towards that decision.

You should look at expression as not just something word of mouth. You can express your qualities through example, even living reclusive. You can express yourself tending to a garden or brushing a floor. You see you can have people brush a floor and get so fed up brushing a floor as a complete boredom and other people will brush the floor because they realize that they are not doing it only for themselves but also for other people and that is using their abilities in an expression which is important to them.....

Quality Colors
Green... (people on the green ray, DP) a lot of mental energy would be used in connection with being *impartial*, not taking sides, being objective in something, your mental power not being used to pressurize another person, but to be using all the mental activity to try to create harmonious conditions.

The use of these words (see list above with quality colors) can help you to find out your own qualities by first of all relating to the color and then starting to use each word as a meditation point. People have found out their own quality colors taking each color at a time and meditating on the words of these colors. You can quite easily do that, find out what your abilities are, and then of course the next stage is that you use them. Some people have 2 colors, some people have only one. Now, having contact with these qualities doesn't of course mean that the other things are not important. If you are using your qualities, then of course the other things which may be weaknesses, you are always trying to use your qualities to bring those other areas into their strength.

If there is something that is obscuring your real potential, such as emotion can do, then often you find a difficulty in reaching or understanding your qualities, and so even though you have the color, even though you see it, that is only part of it. The words also have a meaning in relationship to the color. When you come to use the words themselves, this brings you into another meaning. If you just look at some of these words: take **power** which is on the **red ray**. Power is something we use on so many different levels, in so many different ways, so if you are using power correctly, then you are not using it to dominate people, you are using power as a strength that could perhaps link up to intuition or love, so if you could get a proper understanding of power, then that will also bring you into an understanding of love or intuition, so although these words look to be independent from color to color, or separate, but one really leads on to another.

One of the things you could find, for example, this **yellow**, you find quite a number of people have got a blend of **blue** and yellow, two colors which show up with quite a number of people as qualities. If you look at the yellow you have *tolerance* and *patience* and *logic, precision*. With blue you have got love, intuition, wisdom and perception. Of course if you look at logic, logic is something that you use with your thoughts and often logic doesn't relate at all to *intuition*. But then when we come to areas of logic, areas of logic become illogical, when you are not functioning physically or in your normal thought process, so the illogical situation is what is connected up with intuitive aspects. We can find, if we link two things together, that, often that is bringing us into another dimension with ourselves, which of course again requires time to go into.

If you don't have *harmony*, you can't have *compassion*. Compassion of course also relates to *love* or indeed *perception*. Compassion brings a number of things together, it is not sorrow or not really sympathy, it is on a level beyond that. It brings love or perception together, so that you are not doing something for another person because you expect a return for it, you are just doing it because that is part of your whole process. It can have to do with sensitivity, it can also have to do with what you know has do be done. If you are in some place where you see that the floor needs to be brushed and there is nobody doing it. That is perception, to brush the floor because it needs to be done. You can take it into different areas like that.

If you are seeing as for example **rose-pink** while you are working with another person, if you are seeing it continuously, then of course in all probability it is not attached to the other person, it is your quality color that you are using with other people. If you will accept that that rose-pink is yours, you will draw it back into your own aura-structure and then you will be able to separate that from what you are seeing with other people. The problem is not really deciphering what you see with other people, it is accepting what is yours.

You see, one of the greatest faults for people, that when they are sincere in what they are doing, if there is something there that brings them into their own abilities, their own awareness of their own spirituality, then so often they won't accept it.

The reason they won't accept it, is that they feel not good enough and this is a problem. Because, so many people, when they go into all of this, then you have two aspects: one aspect is, they just go into this and they want to work with people, want to do things for people, but they don't bother about working with themselves. The other aspect is, the person wants to work with other people, wants to do things for other people and they work really hard with themselves and have a real sincerity or compassion for other people. But when it comes to recognizing they themselves in what they are doing, they have a lot of problems, because they don't want to feel way up here, they want to stay on the ground, and so they don't want to feel better or anything like that than any other people.

Through the very fact of thinking like that, they are closing off what they need to be building on. This is a real problem, because it is very difficult if you have a person like that, to get that person, to change, to accept what they have themselves. If they could only accept that they are not going to be egotistical, they are going to move into another dimension, recognizing what they have, and of course that itself opens out a complete new field of activity of perception.

Use of qualities

When you say a person is not in a position to use their qualities, then I am not so sure that that would be a reality. No matter what position you are in, you may not have the means of expressing your qualities but you always have the means of relating to your qualities, and if you relate to your qualities you can bring yourself to a point of understanding that if expression is not possible in that area, it is always possible in some way.

If you are even brushing a floor, you can brush that floor with your qualities, you can brush a floor with anger. It is just how you relate your qualities to what you do. Qualities are not necessarily related to working with other people. If a person is doing everything with a feeling of anger or resentment and a negative attitude towards their life, if they are in such a situation, they are holding on to the emotions, so they are not really in touch with their qualities and if you have someone like that then it is very difficult to have them look at their qualities. The only way to help a person like that is through example - that is a slow process.

You can never force a person to (use their qualities, DP) - even if you had a person in the position to use meditation or the individuality-point or whatever, it still would probably have no effect because they have no contact with what you are doing, just using it as a mental exercise. The real process of helping a person is just to keep showing an example of what it is all about. And sooner or later the example will show, even if it doesn't show on the surface physically.

You know as well as I do that often when we see things that are happening, we don't register, we don't express what we have taken in, so at some time it will turn up later and that is the only way you can show a person, just by keeping an example - sometime that will mean something to them when they are in the position to accept it. That is the only way I know of.

Some people, when they get a pain in the body, then they get a reflection in the aura, it may be a reflection of color or something. That means that that reflection from the body into the aura is showing that person something that is related to blockage or something happening in the aura which is related to the pain, but which is not moving. If you have such situations and you can move from the pain to that point in the aura then you can go through it. That would mean that you would be releasing the emotional content of the pain and releasing the astral trap-situation or what emotionally, astrally is held there. That means that you would be moving from the body, coming out of the body and this is where it can be really valuable to have the sense that the causal aura is here, related to the ID-point, that you can draw on that any time, no matter what situation you are in.

If you have built up the contact with the energy from the ID-point then that builds up a sense of well-being, of protection or higher consciousness. If you have this connection to higher consciousness and are then moving into the aura structure to a point which is connected with pain, then, when you are drawn through that point of pain in the aura, you may be confronted with an ugly image of yourself. Now, if you are confronted with that and you have the sense of protection or guidance as in the causal area of the aura, then this can provide you with a lot of strength and trust in order to be able to confront that image of yourself and to move through that. This connection to protection or to higher consciousness will be there in the background, and you can always use it or look for it when you need it, so that you are not, for example, drawn into a fear-area if you see an ugly image in front of you.

———

We find that there are a lot of diversities in the understanding of what energy is doing or indeed how energy of itself can work, and so in many areas, when we look at development processes or the use of healing, we find that different people present different approaches to the use of energy and this creates a fair amount of confusion. Perhaps it has to be like this because it is not possible to present, as I see it, a given technique that we all can use in an exact way. The reason, it seems to me, that is not possible is simply because each of us is different and in that difference we do not have the same ratio of quality. We have some people who perhaps are given to more precision in what they do, while other people are placing the emphasis on belief or some factors of devotion and so we have this as a difference. This is just an example.

There are many other differences that you can find in relationship to quality movement.

What we are looking at, in this is the relationship that healing of itself has to qualities. We find that qualities, if they are used correctly, are always for the well-being of other people as well as ourselves, and of course that is true. But when it comes to applying the healing energy of qualities towards another person as a means of making change or helping change to occur in the other person, then we come into a more precise area of using that energy of quality, that healing energy of quality, which is not usable, as I see it, by everyone. We can say that everyone has a degree of healing means to help other people, but that may not produce the strength that is needed at a particular point of time. When we view the whole area of healing, then we can find some people having this degree of quality that reflects more strongly the healing agency towards another person or other people.

Is the cause of illness related to separation of the human being from their quality area and I wonder when that separation happens? Perhaps it happened in the Garden of Eden. There is no doubt, the way I see things, that there is a separation between qualities and some people's abilities to allow those qualities to be used. There are many people where you don't see vibration in their qualities. With many people the quality vibration is almost still.

We can see this in another way too. Sometimes we can see people and they may look very fine physically, but when we start to go into the relationship they have to their own mental conduct then it is almost as if there are physical changes. I have seen some people with hands that have been almost like claws and that is simply because their mental activity is grabbing and they want everything for themselves and so, what they use their hands for is to do that, so the hands become a symbol of just grabbing things from other people. That is their mental attitude related to their physical body or how they use their physical body and of course in such a situation there is no contact with their qualities.

And so, when we talk about this original point it would seem to me that there must have been a point wherein something created a division or separation between a person's conduct related to their qualities and how a person relates towards other people. To me the Garden of Eden has always been symbolic, symbolic of what can be looked on as an elemental process seen in the serpent, which affected the emotional or the greed aspect of Eve which she in turn reflected to Adam.

I am saying that because this to me seems to be where we can see the weakness in the female, more than we see in the male, in the emotional level, and often the female, who is held into that emotional level, can affect the male and so trap the male into the emotional level as well. And then we have the opposite: if the male has the means of resisting that female emotion then that is a big help to the female to help her to rise above the emotion. And if the female has the means of rising above the emotion then the mind-capabilities of the female are tremendously strong and so, in that, then she brings this area of intuition to the male and so we have this circulation of energy.

If this is happening in a relationship then both of those people are very much related to their qualities and in being related to their qualities then you can find there is a blend which may not show up as a physical blend but a blend that shows itself in a dimension that could be mind, that could be spiritual, or could be feeling or whatever.

As I see **polarity**, each of us have polarity in ourselves and we have got to learn to use it on ourselves in order that what we blend with as an external polarity can be a blend that is showing up in a movement between two people and in this way we have growth, because not everything that is related to birth is on a physical dimension. There is birth on other dimensions which are reflecting growth between two people which is very important.

The blending of qualities in healing
First of all, if we go back to that question of original sin, we have to reach a point, if we are looking for a cause, which is outside of the physical. For example we could have cancer that is created by physical causes such as asbestos. Maybe it would be possible for a person to have built up their vitality so the asbestos doesn't affect them, but when we are talking about illnesses that have a cause that cannot be determined in a physical sense, such as with asbestos, we are looking for something on another level to be the cause. So what we see physically is a symptom of the cause.

If healing is going to be working correctly then it is always the cause that we are looking for, or to change what has created that illness. If we are going to be doing that we have to be in contact with an energy, an intelligence that can eradicate the cause. That intelligence has given us, as I see it, our qualities or we have grown with our qualities to reach towards the intelligence. If we are going to channel towards another person who is in need, then the relationship from our qualities to contact that person's qualities, becomes a very important aspect of the healing. That blend then, is bringing in that strength of energy which can be transformed from that level down through the different levels to that person's physical body and in this way then the person receiving the healing is being uplifted to a different attitude.

I have never seen a person who has been cured through healing who have not changed their **attitude to life**, they have always done that and that is simply, as I see it, because the healing aspect has given them something new to understand within themselves. They may not fully understand it, but they are open which they were not before, and it is the qualities that are a channel for this and of course, what may lie beyond the qualities. That would be the essential thing in healing.

When we come to healing itself, the applied energy through one person, whom we are calling a healer, towards another person, that applied energy must relate to the qualities of the healer, because it is those qualities that are giving that healer the means to use his energy on another person, so there is no magic in it, there is no drawing from God in the sense that it is just a special type of person that can do healing.

Everything that we see related to energy is moving through its different levels of connection, which we call consciousness and in that movement then it is using all the relative states of consciousness that it can possibly do to move energy outward, so that from the quality level right to the physical problem level the whole lot becomes merged in the movement of energy of that healing process. So we have no limitations in it.

You have to get more and more understanding of the difference between what is not you and what is you - and what is NOT you is your blockages and what IS you is your qualities, but you have got to learn to recognize the difference. The blockages are not what we see in the quality-area of the aura, they don't even interfere with the quality-area. The blockages only interfere with the qualities being drawn in to be used. So these blockages we are speaking about are the identification of the ego, bringing what you want - if you want something and you don't get it, that **becomes a blockage**, so we have this big difference between WANT and NEED. So the whole aspect of NEED is not related to a material aspect or a physical aspect, it is related to what quality, spirituality, higher consciousness, God or whatever, what that relationship is to you, that is where your need is centered and from that then the whole process of clearance takes place.

Meditation on qualities
The abilities that we all have, that we are born with, we can see in the outer area of the aura - one or more of these colors. They will not change so far as the actual color is concerned. The only change we find in these colors, as we progress though our life, is that the color becomes more refined or it becomes more pastel. If a person is not using their abilities, if they are not doing anything to improve themselves or to work with their abilities, then the color remains quite dense and there is practically no movement, no vibration from the outer area of the aura, where these colors are situated. If a person is working to use this higher energy, or accumulative energy, then we can find that these colors do start to vibrate and so this change of structure begins, as a change in the shade of the color.

.... to find out which of these colors are associated with you: each of these colors are known as **rays**, that is a separate identity from the colors we can see in the aura-structure close to the physical body. These rays are what we use in projection states, or expression-states. I have related these words to each of these colors (see list above), because each color has a particular association with expression. So each of these words has its own importance in relationship to a particular color, which means for example, when we look at the **red** we have the words ***will, courage, power, self dependant and leadership.*** We can find, if we take any one of those words - power - now power is a word that everyone has connection with. Many people want to have power over other people, or power in the job they are doing. The word **power** can be used on a number of different levels.

When we talk about progress in using abilities, progress in releasing your physical hold on energy-structure, so that you are not creating suppression with other people or you are not overriding other people or you are not feeling superior to other people, all these things are associated with power. When we come to power in the sense of using energy or using compassion or using love, then that power is not at all situated in the physical structure of things. It is situated in a spiritual structure or higher consciousness-area. The power that we are really looking for in regard to the red ray is a power of non-interference, of an energy movement that is allowing energy to work without us endeavoring to bring our own ego into the process of that energy working.

With most of these words we have this aspect of the physical as distinct from the aspect of higher consciousness being used. If you are going to try to work with these words yourself, one of the things you can do is to make a contact with the colour get an appreciation of it and what the color means to you. Then you can start to meditate on each word, starting off with the red ray which is the number-one-ray.

One of the things that you will find is that some of the words will appeal to you more than others, so that by going through this form of meditation on each word you will find that you will gradually eliminate some words and put more emphasis on other words. From that you will be able to find which color or colors are yours.

In this way you will get some idea of your abilities. It takes time of course, because you have got to go through each word. When you are using these words: as always, words are very powerful, very important, they are expression and therefore they have a meaning. You should try to use the word orally first of all before using it internally. Just saying it aloud, that can be helpful, just as using a mantra. And translate them in your own language before using them.

Transcriptions by Antje Martin, from early 80's courses

—

That brings us in contact with what many people speak about, particularly at the present, as **past life structure**, or karma. It seems to me that each of us has our own karma to work out - each of us has things to do, to work with, and to perhaps overcome. In groups like this I seldom broach the subject of reincarnation, because I have found that so often such patterns can quite easily become a trap. My understanding has been very much related to the possibilities of using our thoughts in a more constructive, present-day, activity. That is what I have been given to teach. Therefore the whole aspect of what I teach is related to using one's thoughts in such a way as to be open for guidance, or to activity that gives us more means to place ourselves in the present structure of life. And using whatever means our thoughts bring forward, to look at the present, to accept the conditions of the present, so we can learn from it.

This past month for me has been a tremendous learning process. Learning because, when one gets into a condition where a change occurs within perhaps 30 seconds, a change over which one apparently has no control, then one must accept such structures that are there. And when the mind becomes clearer, then to learn, what those structures are giving as knowledge and understanding. It is, I think, within this that I came to value very much the whole aspect of what I have been using throughout my life, and what I have been trying, particularly over the past 18 years to teach other people to use; to become clearer in their own ability to think.

Learning seems to me to be very much an important aspect of living. An important aspect, because the whole depth of what one can be in contact with is not confined to one's physical body. My awareness, related to what took place suddenly with me (he is referring to a health problem, DP) very much extended to levels of consciousness and beyond these levels of consciousness, bringing me into areas of contact that very much emphasised, particularly, the process of teaching that we have been reaching within many groups - **the essence of self**. That is very much the emphasis we've been placing on our teaching in our synthesis groups over the past few years.

To try to appreciate, the essence of self, for me requires an increasing understanding of energy. That increasing under-standing of energy is something I was brought strongly into contact with, again through what took place with me (a health problem). I learned, for example, that even within our physical hearts there is polarity. There is **polarity** that operates between the upper and lower valves, particularly on the left side of the heart. And that polarity is as much positive and negative as the polarity that we've had you work with from one side of the body to the other. This polarity is nothing new; it is something one can read about in medical books - as I did. One does not register that polarity so strongly, perhaps, because one is thinking about polarity that relates to male and female energy.

Polarity is an influential structure that reflects between the nervous system and the muscle structure of the body, as it reflects in the blood-circulation that moves through the valves of the heart, as it reflects in your everyday breathing as it reflects in the movement of your arms and legs. Polarity is a very important structure of your life. When this polarity breaks down, then that is going to create a physical problem for you, which will also show up in the energy fields that are active around your body. We have talked quite a lot about polarity, and we have talked about it, as I said, more in a sense of looking at the activity of energy that one can see or sense or feel around the physical body. But we must also look at what's taking place inside the physical body, and here it seems to me there is an important structure which very often we neglect. ...

... during this past month, I have been very much aware of the activity that relates to the physical body and what is going on inside the physical body, particularly related to the **etheric** that is inside of the physical body. This has shown up to be a tremendously important learning factor.

If we are to get the co-ordination I have so often talked about, of the etheric inside the physical body with the etheric external to the physical body, then that co-ordination takes in the polarity structure that operates within the various muscles, organs, endocrine gland system that is inside the physical body. This polarity structure is a polarity structure that again, would seem to me to have different activities which one tries to understand. And so we can find that there are activities there which relate to how we use our thoughts, how we use our physical body, the influences that operate between ourselves and other people, the activity that shows itself in how we speak, what we speak about, how honest we are within that speech, whether our thoughts coordinate with the words we use. That is all part of the activity that operates within the inner etheric structure, the etheric structure inside the physical body.

There are other aspects of this, and these other aspects have always been something that I've tried to look at or work with in different ways, not really as a means of curing or clearing. These aspects are referred to as hereditary, coming from the family background ...and have been passed on from generations in the past. Again, all of this seems to me to be necessary to accept in order to be able to appreciate what has to be learned from it. It can be the same with anyone of you that not all the things that perhaps go wrong within your physical body are there because you of yourself are producing them in that way. It may be that some of them are coming from your family background. This does not excuse anything, this does not mean that you've got to relinquish your responsibility, for the things you think, the things you say, the actions you use. Rather the opposite.

In the whole teaching of how we use thoughts on ourselves, one of the most important things is to be aware, to be aware of what is taking place with you, to be aware of what is happening between you and other people. ..... So often in groups we've talked about compassion, we've talked about people who are working with other people, and the necessity to have a feeling for what one does....

This again shows to me the importance of what takes place between a doctor and a patient, a nurse and a patient, a therapist and a patient, a healer and a patient - it makes such a difference related to the response. That also involves the **inner etheric** inside the physical body. That also involves the means to establish or to rectify the polarity balance inside the physical body. Again looking at all of this, the importance of being honest with oneself became even clearer.

This whole activity of inner etheric reaction is a very important activity. At some stage you and I will have to die. When you are younger you perhaps don't think so much about that because life is full of adventure, life has a lot to offer. But as you get older, perhaps reaching my age, then of course weaknesses have established themselves in your body, and it is not possible to correct them, then of course these weaknesses, when they become pronounced or something happens, bring your thoughts to what is deeper. What exists beyond the physical, what is there that one has got to try to be aware of.

Perhaps I have been very fortunate in my life, that the direction I have been guided in have given me opportunities to have experiences related to a non-physical level of life. Those experiences helped me tremendously when this crisis arose. It wasn't at all that I was just concentrating on such experiences. In fact, when this… (health problem, DP) took place, I was only aware of the pain: I was only aware of the water filling my lungs, of the inability to speak. And so I had to wait, until the work of the doctors and the nurses over the hours that they worked on me had subsided. And indeed it was only when I came back to full consciousness, that I was able then to start to look at this connection to experiences that I've had related a non-physical aspect of life. But having the means to do that was tremendously rewarding, because it strengthened my means of making contact with that level of life.

Now this is something that is involved with this teaching. The things that we use, the exercises that we do, the meditation that we are involved with, are all related to what we can do with ourselves, so when it is possible, we can reach this deeper contact within ourselves, and that can help to bring us into a blending or a bridging of the non-physical with the physical.

And also have a consciousness of it. The consciousness of it, for me is an important thing. One can talk of such things or indeed read of such things, but to have the experience of it within oneself, now that it the vital factor. That is where the reality of all this teaching is.

I'm not saying that what we are teaching here is the only means to learn of this - it is not. But it is a means to learn of it. I can say most surely, that if you pursue the work that is taking place through **exercises**, through **meditation**, that it will bring you to an understanding of how to establish a better blend between the essence of yourself and your physical self. So when we use exercises, as for example with polarity, those exercises are not just there to use intellectually. They are there to be used with a feeling that will work in exercises for you, individually for you, to help to bring you into a better balanced structure within yourself. It is not to say that these things that we work with are going to make you a perfect person. But they are going to give you an opportunity to be able to appreciate what you are going through in your life, what perhaps is necessary to go through in the future. Most of all they are going to give you an opportunity to register yourself in a present situation, and help you to deal with that present situation by realizing that it is possible, to overcome fear.

Fear is one of the biggest problems that seems to me to affect other people. And so, in affecting other people, then, if you have fear in yourself, it registers with you. Fear is an infectious connection of energy. Fear is something that moves from one person to another person, like depression. Do you know that depression is one of the most infectious things that there is? It's easily reflected from one person to another person. That is where awareness comes in. You need to be aware of your own condition in situations you are in. You need to be aware of joy in yourself.

Joy, as we've said so often, is the movement of love that reflects in the inner self and becomes expressed outwards. Love begins at the solar plexus, it moves from the solar plexus to the heart and becomes transformed at the heart. In that transformation it becomes joy. That is the reality of the movement that one can find if one is working with oneself correctly. One must of course have **discipline**. That discipline is a necessity. One also must give time to allow things to build up, to grow. The discipline that one has, and the time that one uses in that discipline, has certainly got to be connected to the will to do things. But also one has got to feel the joy in doing it. There is no point in sitting down to work with exercises if you're having the thought: "Well, I have got to do these because Bob Moore said I have got to do it" as that makes nonsense out of it. If you want to do something, you're doing it because you feel for doing it.

You build up a joy in yourself, realizing that to do it is a benefit to aid you to live. In your physical body, within your relation-ship to other people, we can get into thoughts of criticising, of judging, of blaming other people. That is very much part of what we can find as the ego. And of course the ego is what so often you find people condemning: 'you should not have ego'. Of course, when we have such criticism, that is not very productive, it is not very helpful. It certainly does not help the other person, but most of all it does not help us as it traps us into holding on to that ego that is where we get support from.

Condemnation is a support for many people. Judgement is a support for many people. But that support never takes them any further than that negative attitude. I bring that forward like that because, when you are endeavouring to help other people, there is no space for judgement, for criticism, or for condemning. You've got to reach to move into a freedom, a freedom that belongs to you, a freedom that is your means to appreciate your real purpose in being physically alive at this time.

If you listen to the radio, or turn on the television these days everyone talks about **freedom.** Freedom is a word which is used thousands and thousands of times. But it seems to me that so often when people are talking about freedom, that they are not really talking about freedom. They are talking about an ego trip to get something as an escape. With any freedom there is **responsibility**, and that responsibility is your individual responsibility. That responsibility gives you an opportunity to find a reality in freedom. Freedom is not an escape from anything. True freedom takes you into a means to understand, to deal with situations. It does not always mean you are going to be successful. But what it does do is to take you away from the fight inside yourself, where one part of you is fighting against another part. This fight is what diminishes energy, uses energy up to tremendous extent. With many people it produces a burn-out, which is a situation where there is no energy left to use in any other way, except to continue the fight that is going on inside you.

When you come to work with **exercises** or do **meditation** there is no fight. If you have established in yourself the thought that you want to do something to increase your awareness of life, want to do something to live in a better way, then working with yourself by using your thoughts constructively can help you do that, but you must be prepared to look at what is necessary to go through in order to become free with responsibility.

In this progress that we have been placing before you each time that we have met, we have been using points, we have been using streams and we have been using activity that reflects the movement of energy that goes on within you and around you. Much of this has come from my own experience. The majority, not all, but the majority of exercises that I would use in groups, I have used on myself. I have done that because it is perhaps the type of mind that I have got which needs to find out about things, I have got to try to understand how things work? Why do they work like that? What's the purpose in it? And so for me it is always necessary to try to use things, to try to understand what takes place in their use.

Over twenty years ago, in fact it is over thirty years ago, I went through a period of meditation, in which, it was a deep form of meditation, in which I got exercises related to working with myself, and also working with other people. I never used those exercises until just before I came to Denmark. I didn't use them because, again, I wanted to use them on myself before giving them to other people. So often in going into a deep form of meditation, I find that it is possible to bring oneself into connection to other dimensions that exist around us, that so often we all are not aware of when we are just holding on to the physical world or our physical body. These other dimensions of consciousness are dimensions that one also can move beyond.

Meditation is not just something that relates to experience. I keep repeating this so often to various groups.... Many experiences that we have are valuable. They are related to reaching different levels or different degrees of contact with yourself or different dimensions of contact. But then we can move beyond that, to **a state of non-experience**.

One must ask, of course if one is going beyond experience, what can one register, what value is it, what is it doing? I bring this out now, because everything in our form of teaching starts off as a preparation, and moves you through that preparation to another dimension, and so it's progressing. Meditation is progressive, and this level that can be reached - I'll call it level as a description – this level that can be reached, takes you beyond any physical thought experience. It's a level that I've called **stillness**.

Within that stillness, all that I can register within it is that one is part of everything, there is no separation, there is no division, one is just part of the whole structure of life. That brings you into something that is quite different. That difference gives you an upliftment, a well-being, gives you a strength that is bridging the world of spirituality with your everyday physical life. It gives you the means to move beyond judgement, it gives you another appreciation of feeling, it gives you an awareness of responsibility which is not just linked to you having what you consider to be a good experience. When I talk like this, I'm not at all minimising experiences that are progressive which are bringing you into more acceptance of your own individuality; so that then the dependency that you may have on another person gradually moves to the dependency that you have, or can find, within the essence of yourself and what that means in moving beyond the experience. Again, I bring this out in the beginning of these seven days. (End of tape)

The beauty that you see in the flowers is not really what you are registering with your eyes; it is what you feel with your heart. And what you feel with your heart is what the progress is: taking in stillness, so that you are not involved with any intellectual structure of analysing or just seeing something with your eyes. The things that are most important are what you feel with your heart not what you see with your eyes.

Norwegian group 1993, transcription G. Hatt

——

Honesty
My development depends on how honest I am to myself. Truth and faith is the reality of development. Truth can only advance through faith. When you are between 3 and 5 years old, the basic religious conditioning happens.

The philosophy, if I can use that word, that has built up with me, I feel for a long, long period of my life, is connected to the thought that what I have discovered related to myself, I would like to pass on to other people so that perhaps it can help them also to discover something within themselves. This has brought forward many things for me. In the process, particularly in the past forty two years, I have gone through numerous changes, some of them bringing me into a totally different connection with myself, how to look at myself and different ways to be working on myself. These changes have brought me into different ways of viewing life in general and other people in particular, having moved from what I think I would call a strictly religious upbringing, to a wider concept of acceptance and respect for other people's ideas and views. This has meant, for me, going deeper into myself, re-assessing some things that were given to me as fundamental truths, trying to understand those things in relationship to what I was brought into conflict with beyond that fundamental structure.

One of the things that played an important role in my life has been experience. It was an experience I had, which brought me into conflict, with myself, with my belief, and confronted me with what was real and what was not real. That experience totally changed my life, changed it in such a way that, after a period of trying to discover something that was different from what I had been taught, I had to leave behind the position that I had thought about related to the church. I learned a lot of lessons through that experience, not only to change from being so deeply involved with that aspect of formal religion.

But I learned something then, in those very early days of change - the connection to expectation. Having gone into that many times since, what I call that original experience that I had, I can see that many people, also including myself in those early days, become trapped in expectation. I learned that one has got to live without building on expectations. When one creates expectation, one changes the direction of experience and, within that change, one can find oneself moving away from what the reality is, or can be, in connection with one's process.

It seems to me that in our lives, one of the most important things is preparation, preparation for the things that we do and this involves learning. Learning itself has different perspectives within it. One can learn as one does at school or at university. And within that, in learning quite often one finds the emphasis being placed and held into the intellectual structure. One can say that intellect is necessary and there is nothing wrong with that. But as one would seek to learn outside of what one finds in a school or a university one comes into another structure of learning, a structure of learning that relates, as I call it, to feeling.

It's very difficult to produce descriptions of feeling. Again, in having worked with people for many years now, it seems to me that the word **feeling** has been strongly related to emotion. Of course one can look at feeling and find that if one follows the movement through emotional conditions within us, one of course is drawn to feeling. One can look at that and say that it is the upper bracket of emotion. It is. But then that doesn't end the connection to feeling. In fact one can say that is only the beginning.

We can be drawn into another level or another degree of extension which is also feeling, but which is not held into the expansion or the extension of emotion. That doesn't mean that one becomes separated from oneself. I think one has got to try to discover for oneself what is progress. What promotes progress? What gives us the means to be able to appreciate our connection to progress?

... I know that as I stand here I get a flow or a number of flows of intuition. Those flows come about because we are embarking on a subject that at that point of time is important to various people in the **group**. That flow comes about beyond me. I use the words of course. I'm responsible for that, but there is a movement that takes place which allows me to be in, shall I say, communication with another dimension or another level of contact from which these words are coming, not as words but as **feeling**, though they are expressed in words. But often I have found that words are quite inadequate to express the depth of feeling that is established in other dimensions of contact. This is what you need to be trying to be aware of as we go through these five days. Not just my words but trying to assess for yourself "What do I find behind those words that is important for me?"

Philosophy then is a word which is brought forward by many people as a means to try to understand where we are in our own existence, what we draw in and hold onto and what we express. Within this aspect then of philosophy, it seems to me that one of the things that is important is not to try to persuade other people to believe what you believe, but rather to try to present what you believe as a real living structure of what you live by. In doing that also respecting other people for what is going on with them, remembering that each of us has got to go through different degrees of contact with ourselves, we've got to reach different levels of progress. Some perhaps can move along faster than others. Perhaps if we look at the overall situation we all move very slowly. Philosophy is bringing us into connection not just with a religion that can be part of the philosophy, but with the reality and perhaps most of all the permanency of what life is.

Some things remain with us from our childhood. I know that many seek and perhaps need to make changes in what has taken place in their childhood. And I'm sure that the various ways that is tackled can be very worthwhile. But then there are also some structures that are important for us to examine, to learn from and that become and remain part of our expression. In this movement through life these things that have deeply affected us that we have held onto, that stand the test of time, these are the things that can support us through our lives.

Perhaps one of the problems which I have found with some people, particularly when I was talking with people indivi-dually, is that many people have become dissatisfied with the beliefs that they had or were given in childhood and are looking for something new. Hence the New Age as it is called. But yet it seems to me that sometimes such people have not really dealt with what they were given in childhood. They have not looked at it, recognised it. As they have not been able to distinguish between what is worthwhile holding onto and what is necessary to disregard, confusion arises.

Coming back to the question of my philosophy I find it necessary to look at what I was given in connection to the Church. I was given an opportunity to look at it and make a decision whether to leave it, to pick up something else or to continue on with it. That was related to the experience I have already mentioned. I decided I couldn't stay with it because some things had changed because of the experience I had. But then I did not think it was correct that I should just take the whole aspect of the religion I was given and throw it away and say it was of no further use. So I took some time to look at it. I tried to re-read the Bible with different eyes to what I had when I, of necessity, had to read it. I found that there were many things which, in the teaching I had been given through the Church, were overlooked. So I came into aspects of symbolism which were not considered in the teaching I was given. And this symbolism which I tried to understand has meant a lot to me in my life, has given me, I believe, a lot of understanding.

And indeed it's through this movement of understanding that we have this particular group because this all began with trying to understand the very first chapter in Genesis. It has a wealth of knowledge within it but I do not feel it is understood by many people. I tried to understand it in relationship to darkness and to light and to sound which are mentioned within that first chapter.

In this whole re-reading of the Bible I came across many things which I believe opened me out into more appreciation of life and the different interpretations that have been placed on life. The story of the Garden of Eden for example is such a fantastic story, but it has to be looked at well beyond the words in order to gain an understanding of what it is really about.

In looking at the relationship to Jesus, which in my early days was tremendously important, I have found in some of the words that he is reported to have used, tremendous wisdom that surpassed what I had been taught. Some of the things that he brought forward were never mentioned because they were perhaps proving to be too difficult to recognise in this everyday life situation. One reads what he says about, as they term it in the English Bible, the 'single eye'. That is bringing forward some aspects that one can quite easily relate to in development. Again this difference between darkness and light which would seem to me he is bringing forward, is also present in the first chapter of Genesis.

The quotation that is brought forward in the Bible that is attributed to him is that you should not fight the man who is evil. Could you imagine that in this present world? The world is full of fighting and we classify so many people as evil. Yet it is saying you should not fight the man who is evil. How can that be? Again one has got to go much deeper than the actual words to develop an understanding.

At a time when I was struggling to understand, Krishnamurti was a man from whom I learnt a lot through reading, in particular his lectures in Ceylon. At the same time that I was reading that, I was reading another book by the head of the Methodist Church in England, Leslie Weatherhead, who has written a book called "The Christian Agnostic". Those two books were poles apart, totally different and yet they taught me a fantastic amount about life. I was very fortunate that I was brought in contact with those two books because it certainly gave me a means to look deeper, to try to understand what there is behind words that one can find important.

I'm bringing a lot of things forward about myself in explaining this to you. I want to do that without at all wishing you to place me on any pedestal, because again part of my philosophy is that we are all equal in the process that we are seeking, not only to acquire knowledge, but to reach a destination of feeling. That destination is, as it would seem to me, not the end but perhaps it is the destination we can reach while we are physical.

Within this one can find that progress in development is a learning process which we need to continue with in our lives. Some of us perhaps have different mental attitudes or different processes of mind activity. I think for me, and maybe this was because when I was a boy I was so introvert, I had great problems in talking to one person, never mind a group of people. So I spent a lot of time trying to understand some things in books, when I was very young, in very simple, childish books. But that has stayed with me. I have spent a lot of my life studying various things, things that at times have seemed to me very foolish. When I gave up the idea of being what I wanted to be in the Church, then I moved my studies to electrical engineering. I studied a lot and one perhaps could say I progressed in the material world so reaching the position of being the commercial manager of a large industrial firm.

I was also studying the connection to energy in my twenties, a long time back. That period was an opening period for me in relation to energy, trying to understand energy in the various forms in which one could find it. In trying to understand it, I did many different things. I spent many hours a day studying, first of all related to my job and then related to development through energy. I bring this out because my whole approach, also at the present time, to doing something with energy relates to this study. It is possible to study what the effects of energy are, what one can do with energy and where it draws one to in the connection to oneself. I realise that not everyone has the mind for doing that but everyone has the means of being able to analyse for oneself what one hears.

"Sound, Silence, Stillness." Sept. 1996, transcr. C. Schonauer

—

The laws of life : The law of truth, the law of attraction, the law of cause and effect, the law of love - they are part of the free movement of energy and we must let them work in our lives. Love is a law that operates in such a way that you and I cannot dictate to it, we can only blend with it. Truth is one of the most essential factors. No one can say they have the ultimate in love or in truth. A lot of people waste energy in trying to change the things they cannot change and not having the courage to change the things they can. When you allow yourself to go into stillness you are part of everything. (This becomes) ...a nourishment.

Protection

You can never protect yourself by closing yourself off: the reality of protection is to allow your energy to move outward; when you can do that, you have control over your energy, and that's the surest way to protect yourself.

In our understanding of energy we have got two aspects that we have in most things that we relate to. The aspect that is emphasized a lot is the aspect of **giving**. Giving has its association with what we find in the outer area of the aura structure, and this, if it is allowed to operate, then can be utilized through the physical body, especially in connection with the heart area. If this energy is given correctly, then we don't experience the **tiredness** that one can experience when one is giving just from a physical level. Most of us probably know that, but yet, you may have found sometimes when you are working - working perhaps with other people - that you feel tired after having worked on some people. The reason this comes about is, because in your giving you are allowing an emotional aspect of yourself to interfere with the flow that is coming from the outer area of the aura or the individuality-point.

This emotional interference is registered in distinctly three areas: the hara area of the body, the solar plexus and the heart. If we get this emotional interference which can of course be an interference of like and dislike of the person you are working with, or objecting to something they are doing, this produces a physical tiredness.

The other aspect is of course **receiving**. Receiving is tremendously important, but many people have no idea at all how to receive energy. Many people, for example, have great difficulty in receiving a present, even a physical present. Now, to learn how to receive is just as valuable as learning how to give. Receiving is part of the whole process of giving, because we have this connection between higher consciousness, the ID point for example, and the physical body.

Within the process of giving and receiving we are finding within ourselves that the whole circulation of energy comes into these two categories, that the higher aspect of ourselves gives to us physically, but we have got to learn how to receive that energy that we are being given physically. The giving outward from what we receive produces an effect within us which we call experience, and that experience relates again back to where we have obtained the energy from, the individuality-point or the higher consciousness.

So, that higher consciousness, in producing its energy again to the physical, is producing impression or intuition, or is giving something of a higher conscious nature through the physical body as an expression. This whole concept of energy movement, a two way circulation, is part of each of our processes each day in everything that we are doing in this physical life. We give and we receive continuously. In this giving and receiving the giving part is what we all want to do. If you ask anyone what they want to do with their lives, 99% say: "I want to give something to someone, I want to help someone". But you see, it is not really possible to help as you need to help, unless you learn how to receive yourself! When we look at giving and receiving, apparently they are opposites, someone giving you something, you receiving. It looks as if there are two opposites; however this is not the reality.

Polarity. This is exactly the same when we look at the process of energy. A point here, a point there seem like two apparent opposites. Eliminate one of these points, what do you have? Unbalance. In everything that you find in energy there are apparent opposites. But when you bring those opposites together then you have combination. For example: if I want to draw a straight line and say that one end of that line is positive and the other end is negative, so we stand on this line and say: there is negative and there is positive. But there is a line joining negative and positive, so we have something bringing negative and positive together.

Now, that point where negative and positive comes together is the point of neutrality, not concerned with negative or positive, not concerned with what you are looking on as good or bad, it is just neutral, it is just A STATE OF BEING. That state of being is what I am talking about in working with people, where you get into a process within yourself or a centring within yourself which is not being affected by your emotion of like or dislike.

—

Often the etheric is so closely related to a problem in the physical that it is very difficult to detect a **change** in such a short period, often the change is going on between the etheric and the physical in such a way that you may not detect it until some hours after you worked on the physical level. The change may occur, maybe a movement of energy, but the blockage itself may not be moved for some time.

When you are working in the aura structure you are creating a movement related to something that has been pushed out into the aura structure and has not yet come back to the physical and so it is easier to detect. If you are in a close connection to the physical, where the etheric is, of course you are often working with the physical vibration or the lower vibration that is there on the physical body which you can detect but not really detect the change in it. You can detect the difference but it is very difficult to detect the change that you are making with the difference. That is the big difference between working in the aura-structure and on the physical body, but that doesn't minimize the work on the physical body.

———

If I were working in a person's aura structure I would never use **music.** The reason I wouldn't use music is simply because if you have a person who is trying to work through some emotions, then music would be creating a hold or a trap position for the person astrally and so it would be difficult to get a movement of energy to take that person beyond what they are holding on to related to the music. Using music in healing would be something, as I would see it, that you would use as a separate identity, perhaps to create the right condition or to allow the person to relax, so that you could work after the music is finished. We have in sound then a wide area that can be used in a number of different ways.

———

The reality of all of this is not to copy anyone else but to go by your own feelings, because everyone has the ability to feel vibration, no matter who they are. Even a child with special needs has the ability to feel vibration because it is feeling. Everyone has that sense, and when you can allow that to be your guidance and no matter what everyone else says, if you can just stay with that, then although you may not apparently have as much knowledge as someone who is writing a book, at least the knowledge that you have is true knowledge to you, because it connects with your feelings.

———

So often we can find that we have a division in ourselves between what is happening in the **three lower chakras** and the chakras above. Many people even bring out that division when they talk about spiritual things or when they talk about a higher spiritual consciousness. They don't know how that spiritual consciousness could operate through the three lower chakras, simply because they look on what happens with energy in the three lower chakras as being debased when they compare it with spirituality. This is not my understanding of spirituality.

My understanding of spirituality is that we have got to allow a light source or a higher consciousness source to operate through all the chakras, so that all the chakras become blended. Then we don't distinguish between such things as sexuality and spirituality. As I see it, the reality of the whole situation is that when we express sexually, we can also express spiritually through the activity of sexuality, and we can do this through every activity that we have. I don't see any value in talking about things in a spiritual context if that cannot operate through the physical. I don't see how we can divorce such things related to universal consciousness or universal mind from the things that we do physically.

This brings in the three lower chakras. This is why for me **transmutation** is tremendously valuable, because it allows us to use for example the instinct energy, energy that is an instinct drive that we all have, just as animals do. They don't have the means of transmuting it as we do. We can transmute that into a more controlled situation by moving that energy upwards so that allows what is happening in the ID point for example, to be absorbed into all the functions that relate to the various consciousness states that show through the physical body.

So, in the chakra position, these chakras to me are something of the reality of stages of expression or progress in existence, so that each chakra represents a particular facet of our evolutionary stage.

Chakras are there to draw energy in and that energy has got to be expressed, it has got to move outwards, it has got to make contact with some things that we are relating to. If we close a chakra off, if that where possible then of course that facet of ours could not be expressed towards the objective. In my opinion it is not possible to close a chakra off, we can do various things with the chakra in order to have it balanced with other chakras or to open it out. In the realization that all of this energy is part of our whole heritage, is part of our complete birthright to use, therefore the chakras are distri-bution points of that energy. So what we do with the energy that is moving through these chakras is also very important in what we are trying to achieve in our lives or what we are trying to work with through our lives. So in using or linking with each chakra, that chakra has its specific importance to the overall aspect of energy flow or energy movement.

So when we talk about quality energy or the words that we were using earlier in the day, if those words and that quality energy have a distinct relationship to every chakra, so that we have a correct connection with our abilities, then that of itself influences the activity of every chakra. Then the whole process of transmutation opens us out to allow higher influence or spiritual Qualities to become more used with the activity of each of the chakras. So transmutation therefore, apart from all the things we have said about physical, etheric and mental states also has its great significance in the higher energy or spiritual states.

The **individuality point** brings us into a sense of light. We have used this ID point in a number of ways connected with chakras and we have tried to have you appreciate the importance of what is happening from that point downwards and surrounding our complete aura-structure. When you realize that your quality energy is right out here and all the rest of the aura-structure is inside of that, so if we have a lot of denseness between this spiritual aura and the physical body, then of course the quality energy cannot find its way into expression through the chakras. The more attention we bring to our qualities, to the ID point, then of course the more opportunities we have to allow a better flow of energy through the centre line of energy activity in the spine.

———

What is the difference between the **active mind** and the **busy mind**? The busy mind is preoccupied with all sorts of physical activities or education or knowledge. The active mind is giving you the means to withdraw from that and be passive and then the physical mind is still and the active mind is then drawing in the wisdom or the knowledge or the understanding which you can't make contact with when you are busy with the physical stuff. The busy mind is the interference.

From Text collection of Antje Martin from early 80's courses

What are we? We know we are individually physical. But what does that mean? Here we have got to come to an understanding of what I have seen in connection to **birth**, which I have spent some years trying to understand from an energy point of view. I have talked to you before about having been given the opportunity by a number of mothers, to follow them through their pregnancy and watch the birth of their children, and follow the growth of the children after they were born. That for me was tremendous - to be able to do that. There are many things, connected to the birth of energy which took me a long time to try to go deeper into.

In some of these things that I have tried to work on, has been the connection that exists between part of the child that was not physical, and the physical part of the child. I know that in Christianity, as well as some other religions we are told about the soul. In Christianity it is said that it is the soul that is important and it is the soul that has to be saved. Of course, one can find individuality, but in trying to understand the soul, I came into a problem, because I could not see a soul. So I tried to understand: What was I looking for?

Then I came into something that showed itself in naturalness. For example, before the child was born, it was possible to see the energy structure of the child inside the mother's aura structure. One could also see the activity of the blood movement, amongst other things, from the mother to the placenta, and from the placenta to the child. When one watched the birth taking place, from the breaking of the waters, then one was being brought to a totally different connection to energy. The liver stream in its widening that had taken place - which began around the seventh month stage of pregnancy - that liver stream was helping to create the pulsation that one finds in the contraction stage, or the labour stage of pregnancy. As this was taking place, then as that child was gradually moving out of its mother's body, then the aura or the energy structure of the child became separated from the mother's energy structure, or the mother's aura. As the child's head began to appear, something else came into vision: The **individuality point**, and the **qualities** of the child. Those were in front of the mother, separate from the mother's energy or aura. When the child was born, they became part of the structure of the child.

That was the beginning of the changes that were taking place. Then we had the physical changes that take place with the child, particularly in the heart and the lungs, where the side of the heart which was not working before birth, began to work. That changed the blood circulation in the heart. That brought the intensity of movement into the lungs, where the child was beginning to live on its own oxygen intake. The changes that took place there produced a difference in the energy that one could see with the child. A horizontal figure 8 was formed there which had a centred position in the heart. Each one of you have that horizontal figure 8 and this, it would seem to me from the births I have seen, began when you took the first breath.

When it comes to individuality, there is obviously something that is there, which is individual to each of us. The question is: Where does it come from? Why is it that we have this something which is being called the DNA, which is different from everybody else's DNA. It would be good, if it were possible, that we could regress backward from DNA on a physical level structure into a non physical level. And perhaps we are doing that without understanding it, or recognizing it.

But it certainly does seem to me, that there is something which is there from the point of conception, and perhaps even before that. That brings us into an essence and I prefer the word 'essence' to 'soul'. It is this essence that is perhaps dictating to us individually the connection between what is not physical and what is physical.

One of the things which interested me in trying to understand is birth, as indeed it has interested me in trying to understand death. Often I have seen with females, above the right side of the head, in the mental aura structure, a point or a focus position - a small position - that comes there and then after a time will disappear. I see this with some mothers before they conceive and when they conceive, that point disappears. I also see this point with some females who, it seems to me, have no opportunity to become pregnant and conceive. I am left with the question: What is that point? I cannot say that this is the soul or the essence of a child as I do not know. All that I do know is that when the mother conceives, that point disappears. If the female has no opportunity to conceive, the point can stay there for some months, and then disappear. Maybe it is a point of attraction, and maybe indicating something that perhaps is within the thoughts of the female about children, who perhaps would like to become a mother, or would like to become once again a mother. I cannot answer that.

All of this structure that I am bringing forward to you, all this has a relationship to energy. What it means we can only conjecture about. As there are many things in connection to energy which we do not really understand. It seems we have not evolved sufficiently, or opened out, or accepted sufficiently to gain that understanding.
Norwegian group 1995, transcription, G. Hatt

Taoism is closely associated with higher levels of wisdom, connected with higher levels of mind and levels of divine purpose. This is why I was attracted to it. The meridians play a predominant part in the physical/etheric structures. They are the vehicle for energy movement, for creating an impact in an individual process into the Divine. This involves a deep understanding of the human nature, of the feminine and masculine energy. The points we are working with are merely focus points for the energy movements we are working with. These points are revealing and telling us a lot about the Individual. You see, there is a higher level to polarity that is not revealed yet to Mankind. We must first get through the denser areas in order to understand these higher levels of polarity structure. I admit it is not an easy process. This requires willingness and patience to understand yourself. Honesty is one of the major foundations in this way of working. If you are dishonest to yourself, to other people, you cannot break through to yourself and cannot benefit from this polarity within yourself. I have been trying to teach this the best I could while being physical.

From a channelling through Eva Høffding, January 2012, when I asked Bob about how much his psychic streams were inspired by Taoism.

———

Stop searching for light and accept what is happening with you at any point of time. When you are placing so much emphasis on something that you are aiming for, you are missing a lot of other things, and the reality is to remain in the present and accept everything that is going on in the present, so you are not drawn away from yourself into complications of other people's wants or desires or closed minds or whatever.

As in all **development** there has got to be a state of progress. The progress is not just related to doing exercises. The progress in development is also related to understanding the response of energy. That invariably means getting a better understanding of yourself. But of course, to get understanding of yourself is not the easiest thing to do, because there are many factors which tend to prevent us from getting an understanding of ourselves, and not least of these factors is what we want to hold on to.

We may get some glimpses of another type of understanding from what we are generally using, but those glimpses of themselves often create fear or hold us more into this center part of the body, simply because we recognize that if we are to do something different from what we have been used to doing, then that means us taking away some of the props that we have, props like, anger, fear, self-pity. Those are old props that we use at different times to fall back on, because we can't or don't want to meet up with ourselves.

Often it is not possible to deal with a situation that is showing like this, to deal with it in a direct way, so that when we come to deal with some aspects that are showing up the difference between holding on to something, releasing it, and getting something else, that means us making quite a lot of change in our life activity.

When we look at all of this process of working with ourselves, when we look at the aspects related to development, opening out ourselves, or getting a means of using the sensitivity or psychic ability, now, such processes do require us to release things that we hold on to in a more emotional or physical structure.

Bob Moore – Feelings are the pathway to your soul

Someone once said that the reality of living is first of all to look for yourself and then to find yourself and having found yourself then loose yourself again. Now you see, if you go looking for your self, often you cannot find yourself in your initial contact with other people, because that initial contact you have so obscured or placed masks in your contact between yourself and other people, that when you look there you don't see the reality of you. You see what you have structured, because you don't want the reality of you to show, or you don't want other people to see what you consider to be your weaknesses. Many men, this is changing now but many men would not have cried in front of other people, as that would have been considered a weakness and this is the type of thing that we find, in many different dimensions when we come to the contact between ourselves and other people.

When we are looking at what we are presenting to other people we should ask ourselves whether that is a cover up or a reality. And, as I said, so much use of the emotions has become a reinforced cover up of what we really are. And so, to find ourselves, we have got to be doing things that give us the opportunity to look beneath what we present.

This process is not easy, it takes time. But having found some aspects that bring us more into an understanding of our purpose or our relationship to the universe or whatever, then of course the next part leads behind the ego content, to lapse (give up) ourselves, to surrender. In doing that we have another part of the process, which is meaning for us that we have got to be in the present, not somewhere in the past, not somewhere in the future, but in the present. Now again, you just consider yourself, you look back over the last few days, just look what in those days has been in the present related to the past, what are you looking for in the future, where are the distractions? The distractions are not in the present, they are in what you have structured in the past, or what you are structuring for the future. To remain in the present is of course one of the best means to help you to overcome your emotions and that means being responsible for your own activity.

You cannot take on the responsibility of other people. You try to help other people, but in trying to help them you cannot get emotionally involved with them. You have got to try to give them of your wisdom and leave it at that. That means being in the present, not taking on what belongs to other people.

In this situation that I have tried to describe, the bottom area of the body and the top area of the body are two areas which need to be positive, as it were, in their activity. They become negative simply because the space in between is over active with anxiety, fears and worries, self-pity, anger, so that what is there needs to have some means of being changed, and you can't change any of this by willing yourself to produce a change. You can only change, as I see the whole position, by allowing things, such as energy, to acquire its proper rhythm structure and in doing that then, what is beneath or outside of this rhythm structure can be gradually absorbed into the rhythm; that is **transmutation.**

Control is one of the essential factors when you come to make change, because any change that you make in yourself, if you take something away it must be replaced by something else. You can't have an empty space, there is no such thing as "nothing". So when you move something, then energy requires that it is replaced by something else, so if you change an emotional structure and that is a real change, then a non-emotional structure will take its place. That is what development is, what progress is, taking you from one dimension of yourself to another, and that brings me back to what I said about a holding situation as distinct from a releasing situation.

And so this center part of the body represents for many people a holding situation, but it can be changed to become a transmuting situation. If we are going to change it, we have got to have a better contact in a controlled way with what there is in the bottom area of the body, and what there is in the top area of the body. The quality energy, the relationship to the individuality point must find a means to make its impact through your expression. It can not have that impact, it can not find this means of expressing through your solar plexus, it has got to use other chakras, which are more in keeping with your qualities, and of course the obvious connection with that is the heart.

The **root chakra** is one of the basic chakras of balance, gravity, root situation, of course that will also come into the function of qualities and of course the pineal, the -as some people will have it - 'eye of the soul', is the higher imagery contact, the perception stage that you reach when you have your contact with your qualities. So, the movement that shows up from the bottom area of the body to the top area of the body, in the development movement, has got to become more and more free, so that what is going on through the solar plexus is an aid to your whole process of expressing, so that you are overcoming that restrictive part in the center of the body, seen between the 4th and 7th dorsal vertebra.

Emotions have thought processes linked to them and emotions will always want to keep you under their control, and so this is what I am continuously saying to people: the solar plexus level produces imagery, that is emotional imagery, and that emotional imagery, when it is related to fear, turns in on ourselves and produces something to hold us. The only way I know of to go through this, is to just to go through it, to accept that that is what is happening but to try to maintain the contact with whatever **motive** you had in the beginning for starting the process of development or healing, because it is that which is going to draw you through it. But emotions are tremendously strong and will do all sorts of weird things to trap or hold you.

Many people talk about spiritual realization and many people look for it, but the reality of the situation is that not everyone has the means to accept spiritual realization. That is really worth thinking about, because everyone is talking about wanting this contact with **higher consciousness** and wanting all sorts of things to come from that. You have to be prepared for that to happen, because if you were open to all the intensity of **your qualities** you would not be physically alive now, because you could not absorb the increase of that energy. So the whole process of a spiritual realization is a gradual process, reaching a point where you can absorb what is being drawn into you in an increasing effect.

The discharge of emotional energy is part of the whole process of living. The acceptance of that is to be able to rise above the consensus of **good and bad**. I realize when I am saying this that most of us will want to say: "But we want to have the things that are good and we don't want to have the things that are bad!" But now, when you look at all of this, good and bad, there can be changing factors in it and those changing factors are as important as what you are terming good and bad. I was trying to explain, you remember, the situation in the physical body, where everyone looks at negative and positive but so few people look at the neutral position. And the neutral position is the most important position. The negative and positive are structures that we can relate to as bad and good. Equally they are structures that are necessary to allow a continuity to take place, but when we move beyond that continuity then we are in a different connection with ourselves, we are no longer concerned with the structures that are needed in that particular dimension.

This is what we find in the whole reality of energy: once we bring things into "good" and "bad" aspects in that sense, we minimize our own means to grow. I have talked often about the left hand path as distinct from the right hand path. The left hand path is a reality and the reason it is a reality is because people make it a reality. People want to have power, people want to manipulate other people, people want to use their emotions to have other people scared and so you have this manipulation of energy, but it is still the same energy, but it is being manipulated in such a way as to produce an ego type effect.

When we come to the right hand path, then we have a movement which is an inner movement and this inner movement is also seen as it is expressed outward. The inner movement is a drawing within, and that drawing within is also an expression outwards. This concept of the movement of energy, or the growing state that we find in development, is a consciousness that is not, as many people look on it, working with a **psychic** to obtain something that is spiritual. That is a

106

wrong consciousness. The reason I am saying it is wrong is because you can see so many people who are working with psychic faculties and are never going to get beyond that because they have trapped themselves in that position.

The reality of development is to do - and I have to quote the Bible here – is to do what Mr. Jesus said: you have got to find the kingdom of heaven in yourself. That is the only place where you can start and I am not talking religion when I say that. I am talking about reality in using energy, because it is only when you have this contact with the inner self that the outer awareness becomes a movement outward, so that the contraction and expansion is continually operating from what you are finding within and what you are expressing without. This does not take any concern for what we have as dis-charge of energy, emotional energy. It is only concerned with giving and in the giving it is not concerned about return, it is just concerned about the actual process of giving, and that is what **compassion** is all about.

You cannot be selfish if you want to develop, and the whole development process demands that you are getting the means of looking on other people as also being in a development process, even though they seem to be in a much slower or lower state of development than yourself. This is one of the real purposes in development: that you are beginning to see other people in a process towards perhaps a state of progress that you have... (in yourself, DP) so that you cannot use other people for your own development. It is only in the giving that you have freedom, you cannot have freedom if you are grasping everything to yourself. Any freedom that is related to development is a giving.

In so many things that you work with, one of the things that is important is **patience**, giving things time, not trying to predetermine ... , allowing the natural movement of energy to function. Of course that also comes into the area of acceptance. Often you are confronted with a situation that you try to work with or do things about, and then it reaches a point where you realize that it is no longer possible to make a change in that situation. So then, to release that situation you are releasing it into another dimension, so the other dimension itself then takes over.

In our everyday life context one of the important aspects between people is to try to understand each other. This area of understanding is not always easy, often it is very difficult. But that still does not take away from the need to understand. The need to understand cannot be based on something that changes from one minute to the next minute. The need to understand another person or other people is in reality based on understanding yourself and to understand yourself, of course, means working on yourself. And working on yourself means going deeper, looking at the different states of consciousness, the different degrees of contact that you have with yourself, and above all, learning to like yourself, **to love yourself.**

Of course we can look at this in two ways. Many people can look at this situation of liking yourself or loving yourself in a way that brings it into an ego aspect, but of course that aspect is a selfish aspect and that is not what I am talking about. Liking or loving yourself is being able to release yourself from the structures which bind you, hold you into an illusion. An illusion which does not allow you to see or understand yourself as you wish to, which prevents you from seeing your balance or your flow of energy with another person or other people.

So many of us get held into past situations, into things that have gone wrong, things that we wanted and could not obtain, things, where our contact between ourselves and another person has been disturbed because of our own projections. All these things trap or hold us to the past, but we have got to move from that. If we are going to progress we cannot be held in the past.

If you look at the whole aspect of what there is in **creation**: creation moves through the cycles of activity that we see operating through the seasons of the year, and so we move from one season to another season. If you look at nature, nature is not held into one season, it keeps moving through the seasons. When we can learn to leave behind the things that we should not be carrying forward, or that we have not learned from, or that we have not appreciated through experience, if we can leave that and be in the present with our activity, then we are going a long way to be able to appreciate what growth really is. This is something that to me seems to be perhaps showing more and more as a difficulty with people who are working through things: that they become so involved in working through their own process, or working through things of themselves, that they are not appreciating the **joy** they can have in any one of these seasons of the year. We must always remember that in anything that we are doing there has to be a joy if it is to become real, that the problems are not US as such, the problems are structured or created because of our inability of appreciating ourselves as ourselves.

Working with symbols like triangles or squares that are representing the balance of activity in our lives, gives us the opportunity to appreciate a different perspective or a different level of contact that we can derive from what we are doing in an everyday life situation. But of course in all of this other people help us a lot. We can never develop by ourselves, everything must relate, of course, to what we experience. But when you look at what experience is, experience always relates to other people. Every part of your **development process** relates to other people, not just to an introvert you.

When we talk about an increase of spirituality we also have a parallel structure of an increase of **denseness.** That is not generally recognized, but it is there, and this parallel structure is one of the things needed in order to appreciate differences. In the whole formation of the structure of energy we have these two predominant states, and the two predominant states run side by side. This process is of course what many people look on as the distinguishing factor between good and evil. It shows itself in different states of **attraction**, so an attraction point, especially when we come to a healing process, is very important. That attraction point has got to be within yourself, because it is you who attracts to you the type of energy that you are using.

When we talk about growth or development, we have no means of measuring growth or development in our own process. We can only view what we are doing or working with from the point of contact that we are achieving related to our motive for doing things. Some of you have said to me that you want to make quicker progress in what you are doing, working with other people, or indeed what you are doing within your own growth. It is not possible to force progress. You can only go along with your unfolding or opening as it relates to what you need. And in the movement forward or upward ... you are also aware of other things that have been part of your structure, perhaps in suppression, or the things that have been unbalanced in the earlier part of your life. There is a time for doing things and there is a time for not doing things.

When we are in this process related to this sort of consciousness (while working with the mind body), we must find a means to allow this area of consciousness to function as a control and that cannot function as a control through forcing or physical will. And so this parallel structure, of which, for example, the denseness that has been showing as part of our activity in an earlier part of our life, has got to be moved away from, and that cannot be done overnight. It requires time and it requires us reaching a point. That point that we all reach, some people call it a point of illumination, some people call it a point of initiation. That experience will only come about when you have released yourself from the structures that hold or bind you to the denseness of energy.

When you reach that point, there is a freedom. That freedom is connected with what we are working with now, and so this relationship to the mind body is the relationship that is the intermediary connection, as it were, between what there is in a higher consciousness and what there is related to the chakras beneath the pineal. When both of these merge together and have this means of creating, then we have reached that point where this experience takes place.

Healing in the process of the use of energy in this way is bringing in the means to **discern** differences. This is where the contact with wisdom becomes important - to be able to discern a difference. This is something you need to think about.

In all of this area of working with development related to energy you can find many people working with energy, many people teaching about energy. They may be teaching quite alright, but their teaching may not be on your pathway, and you have got to be able to decide what teaching is suitable for you and what teaching is not suitable for you. In deciding that, it is not you looking at the teacher, or looking at what the teaching is about, it is not you saying that this is right and that is wrong, it is only you deciding for yourself what is related to your pathway within the teaching, whatever teaching that may be.

People get themselves so confused because they go to one course, another course and then another course with all different types of people. There is nothing wrong with the people who run the courses, but they haven't the patience to center on a teaching that is going to give them something that allows them to go beyond confusion or emotion to work with people and with themselves. This is always a problem.

Guides

When we talk about such things as evolved souls, evolved spirits or guides or such like, you see, there has to be a communication contact between such an evolved soul and somewhere in connection with ourselves. This is done through a movement of energy that takes shape like an umbilical cord. In that we have what we will call feed down of energy, or knowledge, or whatever. As I see all of this area related to guidance, if there are such people there, it is their responsibility to do what they have to do. I think that we can so easily get caught in a trap of going looking for such things, and I know that it is so easy to structure your own images, and those can be looked on as guidance, and they may be completely unreal. So it is better to leave that and let it prove itself to you, because if you are open enough to have this proven to you, again I know that such entities have a means of proving themselves to you in a way you will understand.

We must always remember that the **physical body** is important. When we talk about the mind body and the relationship to higher consciousness, of course that is true, but all of these states related to higher consciousness have to get a means of being expressed physically, and that is where the physical body becomes very important. The physical body is the last area of expression, and of course all the energy fields around it, related to the performance of the physical body, need to be drawn to this aspect of higher consciousness. This is where I would perhaps have some disagreement with some aspects of teaching that do not take into consideration the reality that the physical body represents in relationship to spirituality.

The **lower chakras** are there for a purpose and that purpose has got to be realized; otherwise you may as well not have any lower chakras. So the lower chakras themselves, although many people want to get away from those as quickly as possible, but that again is an escape, and so the movement of all the energy from a higher consciousness point has got to be as effective in the lower chakras as it can be in the pineal.

When we come to the reality of movement of energy in development, that movement of energy has got to move from the balance of ALL the chakras beneath the crown in order to create a spiral type effect up to the individuality point. That spiral type effect will not be created until there is balance in ALL the chakras, and that includes the root chakra and the hara as well as the pineal. I am trying to bring into an understanding the principles of working, as I see it, that relate to a complete person, not just separating spirituality and keeping that as a separate identity, because it is NOT a separate identity, it is very much related to all the aspects, including sexuality.

In working with the mind body we are trying to create the understanding that, if what we are working with is a reality for each individual, it has got to be reality in the sense that each individual has their own means of keeping a contact with the earth. That is why I keep emphasizing about the lower chakras, because you can find that some people in some states in meditation for example, do things in such a strong way, that they produce their own unbalance, their own unreality, and that becomes a spaced out situation and so there is no means of controlling that.

It is possible to be using the pineal not from a growth area but from an area of just using an activity that doesn't bring in higher consciousness, and so this is the forced aspect of the **psychic**, which of course is quite limited. It doesn't allow a person at all to appreciate qualities, and so often you can find people using the psychic, maybe talking about qualities, but they really haven't had the connection with qualities. Something is needed to allow that connection to be brought in or to influence the structure of using the energy, especially in seeing an aura structure.

In working with this area of mind activity there is, and this should never be forgotten, especially when we increase the activity of the pineal, which invariably with some people will bring forward the things that are there that are coming into a clearance process. When we have such activity going on and even when we go beyond that clearance process, when we come into the structures of relating more to energy formation or into a deeper contact with another person's aura structure, than we do need a means to keep an earth contact. An earth contact is of course what we call **grounding**, but it is more than that.

When we come to intensify our work with the head area, we cannot do this before having gone through the initial processes that we need to go through, in connection with other areas of the body or states of consciousness. When we come to this head area, we are looking not only at the aspect of clearer seeing, but we are also looking at what we really mean and this will become, more and more evident to each person - what we really mean with growth. What is growth, when we talk about mind as distinct from emotion or physical action? How do we understand **growth of mind**? This is something that is really quite important to look at, because many problems that we can find with people are not in their development process as such, but are related to what they are holding on to, what they are not releasing themselves into.

If you are going to work with a means of increasing energy into the pineal area and that energy is going to be functioning to aid you in understanding, then there has got to be a release from what you are holding onto or have been using as emotional structures. It is in holding on to some things that have been there, which you have been using, holding on to that and then trying to do something to move into another dimension.

Of course, if you are trying to do that you are in a conflict right away. So the conflict which many people have is a conflict of wanting to hold on to the **security**, that they feel as security, that they have been using for a good part of their life, and at the same time being attracted to move into something that at that point is unknown but yet they have a feeling for it. You can't have one foot here and another foot over there, because, if you move your legs farther apart then you will fall.

I am bringing this out in this way because when you come to the mind area, the mind area has got to surrender to what you can **trust** in or have faith in or believe in. I don't know of any other way to establish your contact with growth or understanding. You have got to be able to look at some of the things that you have been using as your props, because those need to be erased. That doesn't mean that from one day to the next you have to release the whole lot, but you have got to be able to move from some of the things to take up something different, so that **surrendering** to your purpose related to what you are doing then becomes important.

When we work at this level or in this depth (mind level) it is not easy for some people. I mean, if you have been in a situation where you have been doing a lot of things, or have been placing a lot of emphasis on certain things and then you are finding that there is some unreality in that, that needs to be changed, of course it is not easy to change that! But it is not possible in many of these situations or structures to do an exercise to create a change. What has to happen - and this is why objectivity is important - when you are drawn into the pineal by using a black colour, then you have got to allow this movement to take place as if it is taking place by itself, without you saying you are going to do something to work it through.

This is what I mean with trust, because you have got to get the understanding that there is reason behind your whole development activity, and that reason places you into the position of needing **trust**, trust in your process or trust in your **guidance**. That does become important, because, as you will find, you have got to reach a point where there has got to be **surrender** from the situations of the past, surrender to something. Now, what that something is that you are contacting within yourself or around yourself, you can call it God or you can call it Buddha or **higher consciousness** or Universal Mind, you can formulate your own definition about what that something is, but you need to reach a point, if the pineal structure is to operate correctly, you have got to reach the point where there is no longer this fight within yourself.

Perhaps one of the difficulties that we find is to know when it is not possible to do something or to go through something. These days we have many people talking about going through processes overcoming things, going beyond limitations. Sometimes we have got to realize that some of these things we set out to try to do are not possible to do, either because the time is not right or because we don't have the abilities or the qualities.

———

When we look at these processes that we are involved with in developing, especially related to healing, many people are brought through different things within themselves, confronted with different aspects of themselves and have to really reach a point of surrendering and using trust. These factors of course show up in relationship to balance, particularly with the root-chakra, the hara, the heart and the thyroid. These chakras, the two lower and the two higher, have a complementary movement. The area of the front part of the body, where we have the movements from the chakras, that area is showing quite different in the whole structure of the aura, different because we have the penetration of the chakras. This brings us into the combined movement of energy that we see where there is a harmonizing going on between chakras.

If you have someone who has reached a position in themselves where they are finding more harmony, then this will always show up in this position in the front area of the body, it will show there first of all before it spreads around. Of course in this process we can have one chakra or more than one chakra not being in harmony or overactive or doing something different and of course, if we are endeavoring to achieve harmony, then that which is different becomes an attraction point, so we are drawn to that more than we are drawn to the other parts of this overall area.

Although I always believe in sharing experience related to development - to me it is always tremendously helpful - but then you reach a point where, when you come into a deeper area of feeling, it is no longer possible to share it, because it is YOURS and it doesn't lend itself to be presented in words.

Sometimes we get into situations where we create a pattern and the pattern is so often related to things that we are continuing to do, and so we ignore the things that are really connected with the heart structure. The reality of responsibility is very much associated with your feeling in relationship to your heart expression and that must take the priority over everything else that we set out to do. If we are ignoring a heart connection in some situation, then that will invariably affect other things that we are doing. Responsibility then is not just responsibility on a surface level, but very much on a deep feeling level.

The meaning of the word **trust** is feeling confident in doing something and **faith** takes you into the higher contact with that, so it becomes part of your everyday process. If you talk about faith that will always involve trust. BELIEF is what you would have as a basis for faith and you would not necessarily link **belief** with trust. You could have trust in another person, in what another person is doing, but faith would be taking you beyond that into another level, so your faith could link to what you have established as a belief and so that is something that you should be using each day. You could trust that **something** is going to happen to the best, but related to faith, your faith would be structured in what you have already accumulated in connection with your belief, **whatever** happens will be for the best.

Trust and faith in the whole process is quite important in the relationship between you and I, important because in this use of teaching, teaching itself has got to relate to something that is going to be helpful to you, and the background of the teaching has got to provide for you a means of growing, or a means of understanding yourself better.

I think this is perhaps one of the most important aspects of all the things that you and I are doing together, that the background of what we are seeking to accomplish together is that you can become an individual in your own right. So you can be doing the things that you need to do towards other people in the use of energy, healing, development. You can be doing that in such a way that you have established your contact with your understanding of the source level that takes you beyond fear, that takes you beyond your emotions, and that in this way then you are picking up an increase of whatever knowledge is passing between us at this time. This is the evolution of knowledge and knowledge is not pinned to any one person, it is an increasing activity and this, as I would see it, is the relationship between teacher and pupil. If we look on it like that, that eventually the pupil is going to have more knowledge than the teacher, and within that process of course we have all the evolution of energy. This involves of course you and faith in what you are doing, related to what I am being asked to give you, so that you are placing some trust and faith in that. And of course that also involves me putting trust and faith in my process or my contact with a source, so that in this circulation of movement between you and I and between us and a source, then we have the whole evolutionary process of knowledge working, knowledge that is involved with faith - not a blind faith but a faith that is based on understanding and increasing awareness of each other.

It is the same with you with people that you are teaching. When you are teaching people you are teaching them to help them to evolve, to understand, and so the circulation between you and the people you are working with will be exactly the same as the circulation between me and you. And so, within this structure we are releasing any selfish aspect in the things that we are doing, we are opening out and **surrendering to a source** to become an expression of that source, and of course faith is playing such an important part in that.

None of us can see an end product. We can only build up trust and faith in what we are doing at a point of time, and if we are doing that, then we are moving along the pathway in which there is guidance, and so that guidance is then taking us into a deeper or greater understanding of the whole process of life. To me this is something that is quite important in healing, because so often we work with people and from what we see perhaps we can try to determine what way things are going to go, but then something happens that makes a change. So, there is something new to learn, that we haven't known before. No matter how much we know, we can always see how much we need to learn.

This whole structure of working with energy is a vast field of knowledge and we can only really wonder at the detail that there is in it. When we look at the structure of the physical body we can wonder how it is formed as it is, everything having its purpose in it. When you come to look at energy you are looking at a finer detail. That finer detail has just as exact a law structure behind it as the physical body does, and of course that law structure Involves the **law of attraction** and the law of attraction is what has you here today, or what has me standing in front of you.

The law of attraction has many, many depths in it, many that we cannot possibly fathom at this time, but it is something that is not just structured in a moment, it is a growing facet and it is something that has built up, as I see it, over many lives, and so the circulation of energy is not something that is just accomplished in one life. It is something that is continually growing through many lives, and in this way in this life, what I pass to you is related to each of our growths, mine included, and in this way we are helping each other. So behind all of this attraction we have truth, we have love.

Sometimes those are not easy structures to keep contact with. Many things would want to pull those structures apart. Many things in a person's process are often very difficult to stand back and watch happening. However, that is part of the law that sometimes it is not possible if I, for example, see something in your aura structure, it is sometimes not possible for me to say to you that you should be doing something different, because I know within myself that you have got to go through something. There is the understanding that we can see with energy, the knowledge that is there of energy, but behind all that is also what is needed in the use of that energy. That has got to relate to wisdom and to love, which then means that is not always possible to be urging a person to go in one particular direction. Sometimes it is necessary just to stand back and perhaps watch this person make some mistake. But then, after that has been done, then to be able to go forward and talk to that person, try to have them understand what has been happening within their process, that to me is how love works.

It is exactly the same with you in you working with other people. Often, as much as you would want to, it is not possible for you to get that other person to do something different from what, at that moment, they want to do. So, again, you just have to stand back and watch and wait. But then, in doing that, and they going through it, you can go forward and help that person to understand what they have gone through and its purpose in their process. All of this is related to **faith** and that faith is something that can guide and help you in the various decisions you have got to make, which are not

122

always very easy. Of course, that faith is connected to your heart energy which is where your responsibility must always be situated.

When we look at the different dimensions of ourselves we often see that these different dimensions are in reality blockages or masks of the real self. We are often using these blockages and masks as a cover up of what we show to other people, or indeed a cover up with ourselves. This of course prevents us from using the energy that we have stored etherically, or that is functioning in other areas of the aura, from using that energy correctly or in a balanced way.

Energy has not in reality been formed from a physical level as it was already structured before you were physically formed. Your etheric was already in existence before your physical body. This use of energy that we are speaking about is something that is established as a creative process with each one of us and what that creates in its movement is changing, depending on how we are using our thoughts. Of course **thought** then becomes quite a predominant factor in the whole use of energy. Thoughts that you and I structure are always going to have energy following that structured thought.

This is how we come to direct energy, and of course, when we look at this, we can find we have different levels of thought. Some thoughts are relating to our wants, our desires, ego-aspect, wanting to possess some things perhaps that other people have, or indeed wanting to possess other people. This level of thought is so often related to what we need within ourselves to feed the ego, and so this is where that one level of need links very much up to want and so it becomes a structure of grabbing everything to oneself.

We can also find in development, a level of development which can be seen functioning purely on an emotional, astral level. That relationship to development is not what we have been endeavoring to have you appreciate as that is a level of development which is very much related to the ego, or to the performance of emotion, or to the cover-up of structures that are not of themselves useful in opening out or in a growing process. So this whole connection to developing the area that we call psychic is not a development just of sensing, not a development of something which brings us into a non-physical dimension. That level of development we can do in quite a short time.

When we look at development related to a higher area of consciousness, or a higher level of thought, then the control of that development is not related to want or to the ego. This is something that we keep repeating over and over again, because that is the reality of development, that development cannot be related to the ego. If development is held into the ego, then quite a large percentage of what you are using is **psychic** - sensitivity mixed with your emotions - and so your use of that is a very unbalanced activity in relationship to energy. The level of thought that we have been endeavoring to reach is a level of thought that links to what some people like to call the **soul level** or the **Buddhic level**.

This level of thought is what we find in the function of the **upper chakras**. These are chakras which draw us into the reality level of consciousness that you will be using when you no longer have a physical body. What we have to live in is then this connection to a growth area of ourselves which is seen in the upper chakras. So this brings us to the difference between the upper chakras and the lower chakras. The difference shows from lower chakras being used on an instinct, emotional level, which is often not under control. Alternative to that, lower chakras are being used under a control that is linked to this higher level of consciousness, this level of thought that I have been speaking about, which shows its growth in the movement of upper chakras. In this way upper chakras related to the mind level then become a controlling factor over the emotional state, or how we are using ourselves in expressing from the bottom chakras.

Everything that we do related to consciousness or increasing a harmony between states of consciousness is of itself producing a quickening of your energy, drawn to your physical for a healing purpose. This is something really worthwhile thinking about, because our whole physical mechanism can either be increased in energy potential or decreased in energy potential, depending on how we think or what we do with energy. This is quite important when we come **to release blockages**, blockages that are often producing physical illness or pain in the physical.

If we have the means to draw in and allow a quicker vibration to work, that will increase the potential of the nervous system, will increase the control over emotions, will allow the various systems in the physical body to operate more in harmony with each other. This then is a process that allows you as an individual to work towards healing yourself, rather than you depending on another person to produce miracles to bring about a change. The whole aspect related to healing very much depends on HOW WE USE OUR THOUGHTS.

When you are developing, you do not develop for yourself. What you are doing for yourself has always got to connect with other people. None of us is an island and so what you are doing in opening yourself in connection with your development will affect everyone else in the group. That is why there can never be any selfishness in a **development process.** There has always got to be sharing, there has always got to be communication. This becomes more and more evident as we progress in our development, the importance of sharing with each other, and above all one of the most important things is not to try to push your ideas or your structures on other people, to learn to accept other people's process in their development.

We can find with some people that they want to hold on, create an attachment to their development that is not necessary. The attachment to development is really not getting us anywhere. If we work with other people we don't work with them to become more spiritual. We work with other people because it is necessary to do that, and what comes beyond that is not for us to be saying. That we are using compassion in doing things to other people is all that is needed. All the other things that we talk about or that are there in relationship to spirituality then become part of the whole process, without us doing it to reach some spiritual level or some spiritual goal.

The difference between want and need is the difference between what we can look on as a physical, material concept as distinct from the deeper or higher concept, which of course relates to need and looking at where you are placing the priority in your life. Many people come into development because it has an attraction, attraction because we use what is looked on as rather peculiar words.

People who know nothing about development use words like occultism or psychic or astral; and these words have an attraction point in them which for many people is a curiosity. In being drawn to some form of development so often the person is just interested in developing this something which they seldom understand. They develop it in a way that allows them perhaps to contact an aura structure, or to see colour, or such like. In doing this they become trapped and seldom get out of that trap. They become trapped in their own ego with what they find they can do which other people can't do. Of course they don't realize that other people, who they think can't do it, can do it equally well, or perhaps better, but the other person has not been attracted through curiosity.

This whole structure of want and need is always worthwhile making contact with to establish what **direction** you are going in, what is your driving force and where are your priorities? In this whole difference that we find now in this age, the difference between what has been in the past and what is now drawing us to a future is becoming increasingly stronger. In the past which was the religious era, we very much related to **authority**, to many forms of ritual, to being directed and only allowed to think in particular ways. That era is passing insofar as the authoritative attitude is concerned. But of course we are still left with the background of what brought religion into existence. The changes that we are finding now are changes related to new ways to understand, new ways to think and new structures to base our lives on. What we are doing is endeavoring to bring into focus an understanding of some of the simplicities that there are in life.

It would appear that many of the things that we are doing seem to be very difficult, but the reality is that they are only difficult because we make them difficult. We make them difficult because we haven't the means to attune to what is there as a basis, and so when we start to work with something of course it produces effects or we don't make contact. Such things are there because we haven't understood, and when we do things with colour or symbols we have some similarities between teachers that are bound to be showing, just as we can find some differences.

This is all related to the increased movement of energy that we find now in the world, and it is giving some people an opportunity to find and use their own individuality and that to me is one of the most important factors that we can relate to teaching, to help a person to find their own individuality, get away from their own fears of being restricted, their fears of illness, their fears of authority.

Your individuality is the most precious thing that you have because it is yours, it doesn't belong to anyone else. When you look at the structure of that, it always will draw you into the consciousness that is linking to what we are calling higher consciousness or a force of life. That force of life, as one teacher has put it, is the life force. I am using a terminology which seems to be similar and yet has differences if you take time to examine it. The progress that is now going on, is that we are becoming freer, but in becoming freer we have got to try to appreciate that freedom is a structure that is related to discipline, to control, related to direction, to movement and that is all part of a creative force.

This difference between want and need is something that shows up in so many areas of our lives, and where we place the priority in the things that we do makes a lot of difference, and perhaps sometimes it is worthwhile asking yourself the question: are some of the things that you go through really necessary? Have you created the conditions that bring you into a structure that is taking you through some aspects which are not really necessary, if you would have looked at the need instead of the want? Sometimes we do things and then after we have gone through them, then we place a label on them and say that it was something that we had to go through. Sometimes the only reason you had to go through it was because you drew it to you from a state of want, and if you would have understood the difference between need and want you would not have drawn that to you. That is an area that is really worthwhile looking at.

The pineal is always involved in any form of non-physical experience, but it is not necessary that that involvement brings in the heart, as **the heart** brings us into another dimension. It is this other dimension which enables us to make contact with a person's qualities and so we have this difference between what is psychic and what is on a deeper plane. This difference is reflecting your own growth. You may have sensitivity, but if that sensitivity isn't accepted then you are not in the process of developing. Acceptance would relate to what you yourself have as a beginning or a deeper contact in the whole process of development. That deeper contact is your acceptance of yourself or the connection with yourself in motive or belief or such like.

This difference between analytical process and what lies beyond that, is a difference that can show in what is possible to understand and what is not possible to understand. Sometimes it is not possible to place concrete knowledge into a structure, simply because the knowledge is not related to that particular structure, and so things at times have to be left vague in order that you don't condition yourself or have someone else condition you.

I don't bring some of the things I say to a conclusion, because if I brought them into a conclusion then I am having people center on my interpretation of a particular aspect, and that then is not allowing the person enough freedom to find their own interpretation. This is something that happens with each person in their own structure.

When I say not to analyze when you have feelings, of course you will analyze those feelings because they have some effect on you, but when you go along using this symbol then you come into structures which are not understandable structures in a logic term, and so you just have to accept that. The illogical, as it may appear then, when you would reach that dimension, would become logic in that dimension, and so it is not possible to draw it as an illogical structure into a logic construction, and so you are left in that position for a period. But I think of necessity it has got to be like that, because this is really how we all grow.

A factor people don't really often go into, which is tremendously important: Sometimes, when we are in this whole process of development we may get a lot out of it, and so we feel very good about it. Then we may try to get someone else interested in it, perhaps we do it because we have got a connection with another person. And so often, because we as individuals have experienced something good about development, then we pressurize the other person to take up development or do something about it. Always in your process of development there are indications of this non-pressure structure on other people. You can't dictate to other people, you can't force them into doing things. The position of the center of the head will often reflect situations of patience, being patient. And of course, being patient is part of the whole process related to healing or working with other people, learning to be patient.

In this development we find many facets to open out. This opening out process of course brings us into contact with many of the **blockages** that we have, many of the difficulties that we have built with us over our lives. And of course, to go through these blockages or release some of their emotional contents produces pain, which can be physical or pain which is not physical. All of these movements through blockages, of necessity, demand that we look at ourselves differently from how we have done up to the present. Many of us do not want to look at ourselves. Many of us hide behind the walls that we have placed around ourselves, so that other people cannot see us as we really are.

When you just think of yourself when you contact other people, when you talk to other people, when you play with other people, how much of what you are doing is really you? How much of it is a cover-up? How free are you in your expression? Now there are not many people who are free in their expression. Often what you are doing is presenting your-self as you want other people to see you. You are not pre-senting yourself as you really are. When you get into that state of presenting yourself as you want other people to see you, then of course you are creating an energy blockage. You will not be relating to your real abilities. You have closed off part of yourself. Of course it may be that you are scared, it may be that something happened to you when you were quite young, that prevents you from releasing yourself. It may be that you have been rejected, or you have missed love when you were a child. Of course all of these things are factors in what we do with ourselves in covering up, not expressing as we need to express. It is these factors behind the cover up that we are endeavoring to give you a means of getting contact with. So that getting behind these cover ups is actually the clearance point of how you can be more an individual within your expression.

The process of **development** is essentially a process which allows each individual to access their own individuality. **Individuality**, as I see it, is one of the essential qualities that we can find functioning in this physical world. If we attempt to separate ourselves from our own individual appreciation of what is going on around us or to how we react to what is going on around us, then this is often a disturbing factor or becomes a disturbing factor. We can this see so strongly in the various processes of development.

Often we can find people who want to imitate or copy other people. Of course this is a very big mistake, because, for example, if you have someone who is reading an aura or is talking about colour or demonstrating healing, that doesn't mean that you should copy that, because you can never do things the same way as another person, and another person can never do things the same way you do. The reason for that is quite simple: there are no two people who have exactly the same movement of energy. There are no two people who think exactly the same way. We may fit into general characteristics, but within those general characteristics we can find the individual approach always showing.

As a generalization we can normally place people into one of five different categories and within these categories we have an idea of how they will react to various types of sound, we have an idea of how they are going to respond to the movement of energy in various areas of the body. We get some understanding of their thought processes or their emotional aspect within those thought processes. Now this of itself is generalizing. But then, when changes begin to show with people, often those changes bring us more and more into an individual contact with that particular person, so that from the generalization, or looking at the general characteristics, we become more and more absorbed with the actual individuals themselves.

This is something that is tremendously important when we come to the whole process of opening ourselves out in a form of development, when we look at what we can do in this physical life.

This week we have seen quite a few people and one of the general questions given to us by quite a number of people was: "What can I do in my life?" "What abilities do I have?" "How can I work with people?" or "do I have the means of working with people?" This is something that we can find being asked all over the world. In every country we go to everyone asks the same question: "What can I do towards people, can I work with people and can I help people?"

This question is showing the changing atmosphere that we find with people themselves, where there is an increasing movement of energy endeavoring to bring things into almost like a community atmosphere. We are finding that the old aspects of development, which show up so much in segregation, are beginning to break down. The barriers of culture and intellect, these barriers are slowly moving, so that man begins to appreciate that man has something in common with his fellow man.

In this way we are seeing a movement of energy that is related to the question that some of you have been asking us. That movement of energy is part of the changing structure of energy within you and around you, this changing structure of energy that more and more wants to become part of an increasing movement, to bring into being something more than has been seen in the past. We can find this of course in many movements and with many people, where the structure of **change** is becoming more intense, where the increase of energy movement around the world is more and more affecting those who have this ability to work with other people.

When we look at this whole area of working with other people, that brings us to ways and means of working and what is required in working. We have many different ways to work, ways that show different techniques in operation, ways that link us up with medical work, or with various types of therapy, or with psychiatry, or with ways that link us up with our own means of using our intuition. This area of **intuition** is to me one of the most valuable areas, because no matter what **techniques** you have of working ,they can be very useful, but techniques are often things that you copy from other people, and sometimes you can find that there are types of techniques which do not allow you to use your own intuition or your own feeling.

When we look at what is happening between people, then this movement of energy, which has begun between you and me at the present time, this movement of energy is always changing, it is creative and from that creation it produces. What it produces of course depends on what area you are creating from. Creating, we all do each day, we create with our thoughts. We have somewhere around 50 000 thoughts a day. Within those thoughts we produce energy, energy which is reacting in our heads.

In our head we have somewhere around 30 billion nerve cells. Those nerve cells are bringing in energy, creating an impulse which is reflected down the nervous system, which moves at about a speed of 200 miles per hour. In the physical body there is a complete reaction to what we are producing in our thoughts. Our thoughts therefore become a dominating factor in everything that we are doing. Within this dominating factor of course we have the means to cultivate, build up, express, extend energy, or we can do the reverse. We can cultivate and build up and hold energy. Now herein we have a problem, a problem which we can see with so many people.

Many people go through spaces within themselves in their everyday lives, where they build up a lot of energy towards what they want. What they want is often something which is not possible then to obtain, or even express in the form of communication, so this becomes an energy blockage, holding on to their wants or their desires. These wants or desires are situated within the emotional area of their mechanism.

If we, in wanting to work with people, have a real motive, an unselfish motive, a motive that is not an escape - and this is something that is very important - for many people are involved in various types of jobs (office, factory, whatever) and sometimes that job becomes rather boring. So people think: "Well, if I could be doing something else then I would not have to do this job." But you see: **everything that we do in our lives has a purpose**. Of course we may reach a point where that purpose is outlived, so a change becomes necessary. But if you move from one job to do something else, you should always ask yourself a question: "What am I learning in this job?" If you have not learned something in that job then you are not ready to leave it.

Everything that you do, every experience that you have can be an experience that aids you in your progress of development. This is really a school of learning that we are all in. Within the school of learning there is no escape, because that escape is really you, trying to escape from yourself. This you cannot do. So when we come to think of working with other people, of course you have got to ask yourself the question: "What have you learned from what you have been doing up to the present time to give you enough freedom of expression to work with other people?" Because working with people is a very exacting job.

More and more people need help, more and more people need guidance. But that help and that guidance can not be given from an emotional area, it can only be given from an area where there is clearance, where there is clarity of thought that relates to your own ability to use intuition, or your own ability to extend a feeling aspect that is not choked off by your own emotion. Herein we have something that is tremendously important to take note of.

To work with other people is to give other people something more than they have at the present time. That requires you, who are working with other people to have contact with something that is beyond your emotional contact that you would normally operate through in everyday life. In this function of working with people, of course what we are doing in these weekends can be a very big help to aid you do that. These **exercises** that we are using are exercises which are related to an area of consciousness which is not dictated to by the wants and the physical desires.

The pineal is essentially the gland that you use to **see the aura**. You either see the aura subjectively, that is within your mind's eyes, so to speak, or you can see the aura objectively, using your physical eyes. Both of these states can be tremendously helpful if you are working with other people or using energy on other people. It can be helpful because, if you can see where there is a blockage with a person, if you can see where the energy of that person stops moving correctly, then you can immediately begin to work there, or work with the communicating points that can release that energy, so it can quicken up their whole process.

But to use the pineal you also have got to have an understanding or clear movement of energy with some of the chakras beneath the pineal. The **root-chakra** is a tremendously important chakra in relationship to the pineal itself. Both chakras are chakras of **discipline**, chakras of

control. I am using these words 'discipline' and 'control' continuously, because essentially your development is a discipline, disciplining yourself, so that you are not being attracted one way and another way by all sorts of things which look spectacular and take you away from your main course in life.

There are many different ways to develop, but each of you must reach a point where you decide, this is the way you are going to develop and that is the way you want to stick with. It doesn't matter what other way looks attractive, or what other movements are there to draw you off your pathway. You must learn to stick to the pathway you are on. In this Aquarian age we have so many things being shown, we have all sorts of people talking about and doing so many weird things with energy, but you see, working with energy can operate on so many different levels.

Our progress that we are all going through at the present time is a progress of discipline, although it may seem that we have moved away in one direction, where many people are doing many crazy things. Yet there are other people within this area of movement who are learning to understand and appreciate what that movement really means, and what the discipline involved in that movement is showing us.

If we are going to move from one level to another level we have got to appreciate the level we are on, before it is possible to move to another level, otherwise you are in an area that you have no contact with. It is only by understanding this level that you can move, or grow.

If we create a difference between white and black, then it becomes more difficult to work with the thing that appears to be not so good, and when we bring them both together then we are not saying: "that is black and that is white", or "that is good and that is bad, that is right and that is wrong"?

In this whole prospect associated with development we are of course placing more and more the emphasis on a higher consciousness contact, to try to have people appreciate that the sensationalism of the psychic is not the beginning and the end of everything. The psychic awareness of seeing the aura, or of using clairvoyance, or whatever may be available, is only an intermediary aspect.

The real meaning of development is very much centered on your attitude to what you have as a reality in, for example, the **individuality point**, the relationship between that and what happens in the **heart** area. It is the connection with the heart area - we emphasize that over and over again - that allows us to take things out of a technique that is a pure technique and place them into something that is a feeling. We then find the reality of feeling towards other people, which, to me is most essential in whatever we are doing towards other people. When you come to the realization of what it is really connected with, giving something to other people or sharing something with other people, I think one of the important things to accept is what that pathway has in store for you. It is not always easy to do that.

Many times you are confronted with obstacles or making decisions that take you completely into something else from what you are normally used to, but there is no other way of going, if you are going to be honest in what you are doing. The contact that each of us establish with a spiritual realization, or a higher consciousness, must be the dictate as to what we are doing, or where we are doing it.

The more understanding we get about energy, the further we advance in the whole process of development, the more link of relationship we find on a deeper level between each other. This of course establishes a bond, a bond that with many people may already have existed perhaps through some past life. This bond is increasing, and from this we build up more and more of what is needed to extend out into the world.

———

Light is a reality in that it is needed as a complementary reality to darkness, and what came before light is **sound**. When we look at the whole function of things, sound is certainly part of the creation process and in being so, then it produced light. In producing light that light then became the polarity or complementary opposite to darkness. But in between the two we have sound. Action is sound, anything that moves produces vibration, and vibration is sound, and from the sound then you produce light or colour. The light will always draw you to sound.

In the **death process** sound plays a very important part and of course so much is connected with death, just the same, so much is connected with birth, and so birth and death are the same cycle in every person. For some people coming into the light at birth is a distraction from the comfort they had in the darkness of the womb. With many people, after having gone through something in their lives, perhaps they have worked to give things to other people, then death is a relaxation, a comfort, and so that is also the movement related to light coming in the darkness.

When we talk about **light** and **darkness**, the reality is that we cannot talk about one being good and the other being bad, we are talking about the complementary situation and that is what we have always got to look on, because, if we hold on to this structure of good and bad then we are in a trap, so we have got to allow ourselves to move beyond that trap. How can we do that? Stop searching for light and accept what is happening with you at any point of time. When you are placing so much emphasis on something that you are aiming for you are missing a lot of other things, and the reality is to remain in the present and accept everything that is going on in the present, so that you are not drawn away from yourself into complications of other people's wants or desires, or closed minds or whatever.

In this process of development you have got to try to get another look at yourself in the area of your happiness. We have tried to get you to understand what effect emotion has on you today, now we can take another area, we can take happiness. Some people say: "well, what have I got to be happy about?" Of course everybody can say that. But you see, everybody has **something** to be happy about, no matter how low you feel, no matter how depressed you are. But of course you can't go to a person who is depressed and say: "you have to be happy, you have to be positive!" because they have no idea what you are talking about.

When we look at all of this content of being happy, within that we have a secret, a secret of how to work with our own lives. In this present age we have so many things that are looked on as freedoms, freedoms that show up perhaps, as a lot of change from how things were twenty years ago. But when you look at all these so called "freedoms" that people are supposed to have, when you look at people who are expressing these so called freedoms, do you see any more happiness in them? Not very much, simply because what has become a freedom also has become a means of non-discipline, so that, what we see as expression in these areas, is an expression that has no control or no means of producing anything more than the actual physical expression itself.

When we bring this into an energy state, then we can see that energy itself is never expressed from one area of the body independently. If you are going to express with energy that relates to different chakras, that brings in different states of consciousness, that brings you towards a state of harmonizing. But if you confine that expression through the difficulties that you may have, or the misunderstandings that are there, if you confine that expression to one area of the body, then you are creating difficulties in other areas, and you can see this so plainly in sexuality.

Expression takes many different forms, reacts in many different ways. The problem with the vast majority of people is that they don't express from the area where they have a sense of freedom. The majority of people in their expression stays in a restriction with themselves or are scared to express, or run away from it. The whole essential factor of release connected with emotion is to face up to expression. This is a problem with so many people because so many people since they were children have become inhibited in the area of expression, because their sensitivity was not understood or they were not allowed to build up their own imagery process.

As these children grow older and go through the very important state of puberty, get beyond that, then their expression becomes very restricted to a show. Expression is not a show as it is a means of you allowing energy, which needs to flow from your body, to flow. The whole concept of development is freedom, but that freedom is also discipline. It is not possible to have freedom with development if you turn your back on expression, if you run away from expression. In development expression is one of the essential facets that link up to feeling.

Dancing
What some of you where doing there, when you were moving your body to the music, you were expressing your feelings as they related to the effect of the sound on you. How you reacted to that sound was bringing you more and more into contact with different areas of your body that related to the different chakras, which are drawing energy in from the different states of consciousness, so that in this way your expression was more and more becoming a release.

Movement of energy is precise, exact, but when we do things which are not in a balance, or are not honest, then we prevent this precision from operating. What we do in our thoughts is very important, how we function with our thoughts is very important. We either disturb the mechanism of the body operating with energy, or we maintain the balance that is there, or increase it, if we allow thoughts to be as they should be. If we do something that is not honest towards ourselves then that disturbs the movement of energy. In all processes that you are involved in development, those processes will only operate correctly if you learn to be honest with yourself, they will not operate correctly if you are not honest with yourself!

To be honest with yourself is not easy, because the whole process of being honest demands a lot, but it also has its rewards in balance, so that the exact movement of energy allows your body to work in a more exact way. With a lie detector test you can measure whether a thought is clear or not clear, honest or not honest, so that so many things that we are doing with our thoughts have an effect on our bodies. Working with our bodies also means: paying attention to our thoughts. Working with energy certainly means getting more and more means of allowing clarity of thought, clarity of thought that is not obstructed by what we do with thoughts in a wrong way.

The idea of **meditation** is to reach a point of silence within yourself which is neutral and that is why I talked about the position of being neutral earlier on. Neutral means not looking at things as being positive or negative, it is just **being** and being is a state of silence. It is not possible to get into that state unless you can look at yourself and furthermore **accept yourself** whether you are angry, whether you are jealous, sad or whether you have got pain. When you can accept that, then you can do something with it. If a change is necessary then you can start to bring a change about.

In this process of development we have teachers, we have pupils. As far as I am concerned, most of you look on me as a teacher. I accept that. But I accept it in the way that, if you and I are working together over a period of time, each of you will reach a point where you no longer need me, where you have made a contact with yourself that allows you to be the individual that you are. So as we come to a very commonly used word: "surrender." We find this in all sorts of literature and programs, people want people to **surrender** - but sometimes I ask what they want people to surrender to? You see, surrender, you can surrender yourself to a person or an idea, you can surrender yourself to money, to power, whatever, to me the process of surrender relates to what you have found in yourself.

What you find in yourself is important to you; I can't give you what you already have, and what you have you have to learn to use. So many of these **exercises**, bringing your into yourself, are trying to have you appreciate what contraction is or what expansion is, because that belongs to you. Now, within this we have of course many different degrees of opening out, many degrees of progress. Within all of this we reach different points, where we can appreciate in different ways what has been happening to us as individuals through all of this process. Now, what has been happening to us affects us again in different ways, so that many of you will go through experiences which are difficult. But difficulties are also important, because in overcoming something that is difficult you will have learned more about yourself and probably about other people.

I have never met a person yet who has been on that spiritual pathway that hasn't had difficulties, many of them tremendous difficulties. Always this demands that you put trust and faith in what you are doing and that is not always easy. Many people who have really good intentions are beginning a process of development. When they go along the pathway for a little while and they find a lot of problems, often these problems take away the good intentions that they had in the beginning, so they look for an easy way to work with the process of working with energy. Well, in my estimation there is no easy way. The more people you work with the harder it is for you to keep up the standard that you need to keep. This is why I get a lot of people who ring me up and say: "a couple of months ago I had a lot of people to work with, now I have got just one or two". I always say to those people "well look at your own process, can you work with more people at the moment, watch your problems.

And you will always find there are a lot of problems and you are trying to find an easy way out. If you are going to work with people, you have got to accept the problems, you have got to work with the problems, because that is part of the process, it is part of the whole development that allows you to use the qualities of your energy. The qualities of your energy are for you the most important thing to use, that is the reason you are here now on the earth at the present time, in this very critical time, so that when we look at what is happening with each of us: we are moving along that pathway, and moving along that pathway we are taking step by step, and within those steps we are learning to work in a better way and to walk in a more sure way.

Most of you by now have our program. On top of it you will find that we put a little Zen-proverb. Now that is a really good proverb, it really shows you what you have got to do. It says: "Before enlightenment: chopping wood and carrying water, after enlightenment: chopping wood and carrying water." And that is really the process we are all in, whether we consider ourselves a teacher or a pupil, we are all endeavoring to find the reality, as I said yesterday, not of you and me, but of WE. If we can get into that area of context, then we have something that is of value in relating to one another, not looking at one person as being up here and the other being down there. We have something that can bring us together as individuals to do something to give healing to the world. In this way we are finding the equality, the balance. So, we are not looking for masters and pupils. We are looking for the relationship in the balance of energy-flow that brings something into perspective that allows us all to relate to a **source**, so that, in the surrender, the surrender is not to an individual, but to a source that we can find operating within ourselves, that is the point of surrender. When we have found that and when we have contacted that, then **surrender** itself is allowing the contraction and the **expansion** to show as the balance that is needed.

Emotion of course, is also thought, thought that has held on to an ego situation a want situation, so when we look at various aspects of emotion we come into contact with the area of the physical ego, or what we as physical individuals want, irrespective of what we need. Again we have a distinguishing factor in this that many of us want things that we do not need. In the want area we are using a lot of physical will to obtain that, and if we do not get it then, of course that further increases all the emotional instability that shows up in such things as jealousy. All of these emotional extensions create many varying problems within the whole process of development.

When we speak about development we are not just speaking about sensing itself, we are speaking about the overall process of anyone of us, so that development takes in everything that we are endeavoring to achieve or to work with in this physical life. Many times, when we talk to people about what is happening in their development, we hear them say: "Well, you see, we did these **exercises** for a while, one or two months and then nothing more happened, we got tired of doing the exercises". Or we hear people say: "Well, I did the exercises and I got so many pains in my body and then I wondered whether I was doing the exercises all wrong, so I stopped doing them", or someone else would say: "I got so many emotions after doing the exercises and I didn't feel that I want to go through all those emotions".

When we start to work with something that is giving us the means of making a better contact with ourselves, first of all, that has got to be given time, because not everyone will have an immediate response. When that response comes, that response will produce something different, especially in your physical body, and what it produces as a difference will often show up in changing pains. That changing **pain** comes about simply because all pain is not physical. A lot of pain is astral. A lot of pain you have in your thought, a lot of pain you have in your subconscious, simply because you feel guilty about something, or you have done something you shouldn't have done, or you haven't done something you should have done.

All of those things create energy-**blockages** which register in this astral area of consciousness. When that registers there, it becomes blocked, because you have closed it off, because, if you feel guilty you don't want to feel guilty, and you try to escape from it, but periodically that will show itself, trying to manifest. Of course you continually use your thoughts to suppress it, and in doing so you just push it away, brush it under the carpet. When you start doing exercises, using colour, working with breathing that starts an increase of energy activity, which in turn will be reflected into the area that is closed or blacked out. No matter what you have done in your life, it is there, it is yours, no matter what thoughts you have, they are there and they are yours. You can't escape them but you can work with them. You can never run away from them, because all of those are part of your subconscious. Your subconscious area has no mind to work with. It is a storehouse of all your activity, which registers your good things as well as your bad things.

Each of us has some kind of idea of what we want to do, or what we want to be or what we want to achieve, or what goal we want to aim for. Each of us has that. That is part of our ambition. But that ambition may of itself be brought into being because of the physical ego or because we want to be better than other people, or because we want to do something that places us in the limelight or places us on a pedestal. Now I am eliminating that because that is merely an ego aspect, which itself becomes a forced relationship with energy. What I am speaking about in ambition or goal is what you want to establish within yourself in relationship with dealing with other people in a balance. In this way the goal then becomes operative, and in becoming operative then the movement of energy towards that goal becomes part of your life drive, part of the final structure of movement of energy that we were speaking about earlier on.

It seems to me that, if the reality of development is going to be established with any one of us, then it is not just for the sake of development. The whole psychic potential that each of us has is a potential that takes us either in a wrong way towards the ego aspect, or allows us to be drawn into a higher aspect which does associate itself with the individuality point. Often, when looking at this whole process of development, people say to me it is very slow, that it takes such a long time to be able to see an aura, to use the pineal or whatever. Of course, it does take a long time and, I feel, of necessity so, because one thing which perhaps is more unbalancing than anything else is the use of psychic abilities without control.

When I was working in England, going around various centers, I found more people psychically unbalanced than anywhere else in the world. I am saying that because so much emphasis was then placed on psychic development, and other areas of development which are really more important were not taken into consideration.

Although having left the **Christian church** I still maintain a tremendous respect for what Jesus said which was reported in the parables. There are so many things in those parables that relate to the whole process of development when you look at them symbolically. One of the things he said was that the first thing you have to look for is the kingdom of heaven, and the kingdom of heaven is really a state of being within yourself. If you can find that state of being, that peace or silence within yourself, then the whole process of development opens out in a completely different way, so that there is no rush, there is no need for speed.

That is what the majority of people are looking for, but many of them don't recognize it. People start out in this area of development and they are looking for something in the way of working with other people. In reality they are looking for a little bit of peace in themselves; of course it is difficult to recognize what we are looking for at times. I am saying that because it seems to me that this individuality point, if it can be properly used, can bring this peace or silence within ourselves, and from that, the whole aspect of what we use in energy will be brought into a much clearer focus.

Bob Moore – Feelings are the pathway to your soul

In talking in this way, this is part of the whole mechanism of each one of us, where the emotional relationship between people has a very strong effect on all the thought processes that operate between people. So often we say things to other people that we don't mean, or we are drawn into conversations which we don't want to be drawn into and then have to use something not true in order to escape. So the whole process of human relationships is not an easy process.

There is within this one aspect that remains tremendously important, and that aspect is being **honest** to yourself. Now again this is something that is not easy, but to be honest with yourself does help tremendously in how you are relating to other people, because if you are honest with yourself then your dealings with other people will also be honest. And that brings us to the **Law of Truth** which is one of the universal laws that does not change. With all these laws we have one very important factor involved, which is also another law, the **Law of Cause and Effect**. With every cause there is an effect, and if you are not honest with yourself you are building up a cause. That cause usually shows in stress, and that stress will always have an effect on the physical body, produce some type of illness. This is one of the golden rules if we are doing something towards other people, that we try to remain honest in what we are doing, or honest with ourselves in what we are saying or what we are expressing, whether through the use of words or energy. In this way we can work with ourselves more successfully.

Working with ourselves is something that is continuous right through our lives. You always have to be working, working, and working. I have been working with healing or running courses for up to 30 years now (that was written around 1985,

DP). I still have to spend lots of time doing meditation. I still have got to work with exercises. The more people you work with, the easier it is to get pushed off the path that you are on. If you can visualize yourself being on roller-skates moving down a road pretty fast and someone comes along and gives you just a gentle push, then it is not long and you are lying on the road. The faster you move, the easier it is to be knocked off balance. The more people you work with the harder you have got to work with yourself. All of this development is a process, endeavoring to reach areas of consciousness which often other people have no conception of.

When we talk about **meditation,** this has I feel become a very loose term. Many people speak about meditation and what they are doing in meditation. But really it seems to me that the majority of people are not really meditating. The majority of people are using means to reach a point to begin meditation. But meditation itself only begins when you have reached a point of silence within you. What happens before that is a means of reaching that point of silence. The point of silence is registered between the eyebrows on the bridge of the nose. And from that point we begin a climb through eight other points. Through that climb you then can move through different states of consciousness until we reach a state of illumination. So much of the work that we do on ourselves is preparation.

All these **exercises** that we do now are preparation, bringing us into a deeper contact with ourselves, so as to see ourselves in a different way or from a different viewpoint. So often we are looking on ourselves from one angle only, we don't see the other things, so that continuously we get into a cover up position, or we put structures around ourselves to prevent

152

other people from seeing us. We forget that, when we build these walls around ourselves, we are also limiting our own expression. ...

Many people talk about **protection**. We want protection from all sorts of things that we consider evil and then we forget that there is anything evil going to affect us. We must have an **attraction**-point within ourselves to bring that evil to us. The reality of the situation is that we have got to work with the things within ourselves that are attracting things which we consider not to be so good. One of the best ways of protection is expression. Expression shows in the use of energy from different areas of the body, thought expression, voice expression and expression in the use of touch, all of this so important. Many people look on their thoughts as being "them" and this is not necessarily true.

Often your thoughts, alive as they are, are not always you, because so many of your thoughts are connected with your physical wants, your desires, are really your ego at work, your lower ego, and your lower ego is not you. It is something you have constructed because you have these strong wants and desires, physically towards things that you see. When you have this strong ego and you see something, then the desire comes in and you want it, it doesn't matter if it is good for you, you want it. Then, when we get it, it is no further use to us. Then you see something else and you go through the same process. So of course we have in all of this the ego being strongly dominant with many people.

The ego is associated with emotion, associated with a thought drive that emotion generates. This is what we are trying to get over. We are trying to move from the elemental aspect to the progressive aspect, the upper part of the astral and from there move into the growth of mind, the expansion of mind. Thoughts therefore play an important part in all the things that we are doing. Now of course, as other people said yesterday: "when I try to do something then other thoughts come in and create distraction, or I want to think about something else, not just doing the exercise." Of course this is a problem.

It is a problem you can work with in two ways: if you have difficulty with **concentration**, or memory, or you are not able to have your thoughts staying in one place and have lots of other things coming into your mind, then if you have an object at home, something preferably that has some meaning to you, a happy connection with you, then you place that object on the table in front of you. Just sit down, relax, and look at the object. Of course when you do that, after a few seconds then lots of other thoughts will come to your mind. Then it is not possible just to say that you don't want them. The more you push them away, the more they come forward. So the secret of working with this is to accept all the thoughts that come, allow them all to come. When those thoughts have registered with you, then bring your thoughts back again to the object and keep on repeating that process. If you set yourself ten minutes a day to work like that it won't be very long before you start getting a means of control over your thoughts.

Not all **knowledge** is connected with a teacher. Because I am standing here in front of you does not at all mean that I have all knowledge and you have less knowledge than I have, that is a completely wrong conception. Knowledge is not something that is centered or situated with one person alone or with a group of people - each one of us here have knowledge. That knowledge has been built up over past lives, and that is connected with our abilities. Often that knowledge is dormant, simply because we haven't been in the correct position or we haven't done something with ourselves that we needed to do, so that by talking as I am doing it can often just affect that area of consciousness that needs to release that area of knowledge around you, so that you can make contact with it.

When you can make contact with the knowledge that is already established around you, that of course is helping your whole process of development. No matter how much I talk, no matter how many exercises we do, you have always got to remember, it is not me who develops you, it is you yourselves. And you developing yourself is part of the reason that you are here on this course, that is part of the reason you are physical at this time. You just need to allow all the knowledge that has accumulated to come forward and this is something that anyone can learn to achieve.

There are certainly rules, and **discipline** is one of them, which is tremendously important; simply because, if you don't have a better control of your thoughts, then knowledge cannot be attuned to and cannot be used. In the processes of discipline you are disciplining your thoughts in connection with your body, so there can be a situation where you are at peace with yourself. Being at peace with yourself then knowledge can come, understanding can come.

———

The question has been often asked: who is man? The most obvious answer, I think, is: man is a person of reality that understands his own mind. Mind is the operative process of growth and development and that growth and development are contained within the many processes that we all make contact with each day of our lives. So when we look at mind we are looking at the growth and the possibilities within that growth of ourselves. Within these possibilities there are many things which we can use, many tools that have been given to us to work with.

Within the exercises that we have been involved with in these pathway courses, we have been working with exercises that are associated with balance. We are using the triangle around our bodies; we are using the triangle so as to appreciate the variances that occur within balance that shows up because of our actions or our activities. **Balance**, with any one of us, is tremendously important. Often we can find people looking for balance within physical contacts. The balance they hope to achieve, or the balance they want to be aware of, or associated with, is predominantly connected with the physical body. This can never produce balance. The physical body has its part to play. The physical body is the animal aspect in many instances of the human. We can find many people operating through the physical body, using strong animal instincts, so as to provide a means of their expressing in a dimension which of itself is not changing.

We have got to realize that as human beings we most certainly have animal instincts, similar instincts that we see operating in various types of animals, instincts that associate with the emotion of fear, or jealousy, or hatred or the instinct strongly associated with sexuality, that can be just as animal as animals themselves.

When we come to look at the processes contained within evolution then we see distinct differences between the animal kingdom and the human kingdom. We see mind within the human, evolving to reach different dimensions of intention. Often, within this evolutionary stage of growth we are brought into contact, with some humans who have reached a very high degree of **mind** growth, or a very high degree of spirituality. This is of course looked on by many as an example, something to aspire to, to reach this point of contact.

When we consider the possibilities of mind, when we use this term "mind", we are not just speaking about our thought processes as such. Our thought processes are tremendously important, where we have different degrees of thought as it is reflected through the physical body, as it is reflected through our wants, our needs and our desires. But mind is not just the accumulation of thought, important as that is, mind is also associated with the physical body, and how the physical body is composed, and what that physical body is composed of.

The glands within the physical body, namely the endocrine gland system of the body, are so tremendously important for the various stages of understanding and relationship in the various degrees of growth or development. Within the structure of the glands we have the evolutionary stage which man is associated with, showing its importance. This process of development and endeavoring to understand our own relationship with ourselves more fully, is to me tremendously important, because, when we use such terms as "energy" we are not speaking about some substance, something that concerns other people, we are speaking about movement, thought, progress, universe, laws, all that is energy, energy that concerns everyone of us.

Using such terms as **"energy"**, you are of course confronted with the many ways of looking at energy and expressing yourselves about energy. Energy is not a new term although it is used much more now than it was perhaps 50 years ago. Energy is a term that has been used for thousands upon thousands of years. When we go back to the ancient Egyptians we find that they had a tremendous understanding of energy, where they related to the different phases of man through symbolism, such as the physical body which they symbolized as a dead fish and they called that "kat".

When they went on to other areas such as the etheric for example, they described that area with the term "...." and they symbolized that with the chest and arms fully open to show the involvement or the draw in towards the whole connection between the etheric and the physical body of the energy which surrounds the body. So they progressed through different areas of man's make up, and, as we know, the ancient Egyptians had a tremendous wealth of knowledge and understanding of how to use energy, and they obviously used this in building the pyramids. Energy therefore, or the combination of energy that we see around us, was perhaps better known thousands of years back, than it is at the present time.

We speak a lot about energies in the world. Scientists are working with all types of use of energy, describing energy in many varying ways. But always when we look at this human association to energy, then we can never separate that from mind, mind being the operative function of man's understanding or will or need to understand. Within these functions of growing, which we are all part of, one the important aspects within that growth is **discipline**, discipline where we can learn to train ourselves or to work with ourselves in such a way as not to dissipate energy, not to spread our energies out in too many directions. This is one of the common faults which we find perhaps in present day society.

When we look at present day society, the emphasis of almost everything is placed on youth, so that young people are placed under a pressure, where they have to conform to so many activities such as education, with a lot of emphasis on being educated to do a particular job. Within this that education is often preventing him or her from utilizing other faculties beyond the education itself. When we look at young people as they grow older, then we find in the present day business world that when a man reaches his forties, then his use in business is becoming less and less.

In reality that is working against the whole composition of energy growth. Energy growth goes through phases which relate to seven year cycles, so that the reality of the situation with the movement of energy, in mind, for example, shows up strongly when the person gets to be twenty one. We find in that showing up strongly at that age, that the thoughts, the learning process, the education, all that is using so much energy towards a particular purpose, that we can find so many people become burned out, as it were, when they reach 40 or 50 years of age. The physical body is suffering simply because the whole thought process, being used in such a strong area of concentration does not allow other movements of energy to show a growth or balance.

If we look at what energy means connected with human beings: the age of 49 is a golden era because it relates to the bringing into consciousness of the higher mind, so that at that age the higher mind gains its opportunity to use or to allow man or woman to show the progress or the qualities that they have to use in their creative activity. When we look at what we see with people now at 49, many people at that age are ill and don't have the means to express. The whole thought processes have been so utilized in one way or another that it is not possible for a person at that age to bring in higher mind or to allow higher mind to operate. You can quite easily see this with so many people around us.

In this way, if we look what we are doing, you and I, on courses like this: we are looking at ourselves; different areas of ourselves. I already mentioned the gland structure in our bodies, the **endocrine gland** structure in your body is tremendously important, yet the endocrine glands are the first things that suffer when we use thought wrongly or if we don't use our balance as we need to use it. Physical glands therefore are showing their connection to thought, to emotion, to feeling. Within that connection we are also relating to mind.

We have only got to look, for example, at one gland: the **thymus**, which is such an important gland connected with the whole growth of anyone of us. It is different and maintains that difference right through our whole life. It is larger than any other gland that we have from birth on. When we look at the difference between male and female: it is larger in females than it is in males. That gland suffers such a lot at the age of puberty, simply because it is not given its proper opportunity to grow and expand. It was viewed, medically, as of very little importance, in fact, they used to have treatment either to reduce the size of it or take it out of the body, because it was considered to create problems with breathing, especially with children. This was done up to the mid 1960's, until medical opinion changed.

When we look at the operation of energy, that gland, which is so close to the heart, plays a tremendous part in the well being, and the progress of any individual. It is considered that the thymus is responsible for building up anti-bodies, fighting illness and disease, so that gland is responsible for our means to overcome things which would create unbalance.

Disease is an incorrect movement of energy. So much of that energy, which is centered in the chest, is responsible, when it is not balanced, for illnesses which attack the physical body. When we look at the composition of energy in a polarity, then that energy in the chest area with the female is her positive energy, her strength energy. With the male it is the magnetic or negative energy. When we analyze **polarity** through its different stages between male and female, then we can see the distinguishing factor that operates through all the dimensions that we know of.

The physical female, etherically, has strong male character-istics, astrally it reverts to the female characteristics again and that is her weakest area - the astral state of consciousness is for the female her weakest area. When we come to the mind state of consciousness, we see mind divided into the analy-tical mind (which for the female is not her strength area) and the higher mind area, the upper mind body, which for the female is a very strong area, much stronger than in the male. That is where the intuition is, where the spiritual growth accumulates.

The female has within her whole make up a tremendous amount of spiritual growth if it is allowed to operate, if she can overcome the astral weakness. The male works the opposite way. The physical male has female etheric characteristics, astrally then he moves back to the male stage, that for the male is a strength area, the male is much stronger astrally than the female. The analytical process of mind is much stronger with the male, but when we come to the upper mind the female is much stronger than the male, the male very often relying on what the female is drawing in. This we can find operating in an individual.

When we look at the progress of any one individual, then of course that progress is centered on the **balance** of the male and female characteristics. This is why balance is so important, why it is not possible to just derive balance physically. Balance can only be derived when the physical is looked at in its relationship to other states of consciousness

———

So much of our physical activity is constructed in limitations. We limit ourselves so much, authority limits us and because we accept authorities privileged to say that we can or can not do something, then within that area we restrict ourselves. What you construct with your thoughts is moving, it is activity and it vibrates. So, what you construct you can learn to control, you can learn to move, you can learn to change.

And when we use within these constructions the **symbols** of squares and triangles and circles, there we come into the whole elemental aspect of symbols themselves, because the structure of symbols is very important. It is a structure that moves from a physical conception way into higher areas of consciousness. So there is not one person here who, if you will consciously use this **triangle** that we are working with now, will remain in the same area of construction with their thoughts.

You will change. You will change simply because that triangle itself represents a **balance** of energy, and the thing that prevents you from moving into balance within yourself is your own limitations, so that you have allowed blockages or difficulties or emotional contents or someone else to place you into a set position, and there you remain. You can get the thought that you can do something more with yourself or you can widen out your vision. You have a means of under-standing your reason for being here at this time or what you can do in being here at this time.

All of this is part of the real structure of energy movement. What we see so close to the body are the blockages, the limitations, the restrictions that we have placed on ourselves. What we are trying to do is to move beyond those limitations, so that we can find a means to release the blockages, to overcome the difficulties, so that our awareness becomes more attuned to a deeper area of consciousness within us. This awareness is so often restricted because we just look at things physically, from an emotional aspect, always looking for the difficulties and the blockages.

If we could only realize that there is a colossal energy-field right in front of us, associated with the solar plexus, which is what I call "**energy of happiness**", because it is from this area that we can draw a lot of energy to create joy and happiness, but we don't realize that, because we look always on the physical body and say: "well, within this physical body I have all these things going on" - that is true. We have got to remember: outside the physical body we have also a lot going on.

One of the great difficulties in development is, to get people to look at themselves. That is the greatest difficulty that there is, because people do not want to look at themselves. They want to look at all the other people, how all other people are doing, all the faults in other people, but when it comes to look at yourself: very difficult! If you are going to work with yourself and that work is going to be effective, if it is going to help you, then you have to accept yourself as you are, with your faults and your good points, not as you pretend to be to other people.

When we talk with people about working with other people, we are always saying that people have got to work from their heart. It is the only successful way to work. If you want to do anything worthwhile then what you are doing has got to have a heart contact. That heart contact is bringing you into the area of giving, or release, or balance, or harmony, or compassion, or love. But you know when we talk about love, how can you do something with love, if you are rejecting yourself? If you are not accepting yourself, if you can't love yourself - and when I am saying that I don't mean you looking at yourself as being better than other persons. I am just talking about you accepting yourself and loving yourself and from that point you can extend that to other people. That is a very important contribution that you can make to your development if you can learn to do that.

Constructions are part of our living, but so often the constructions that we achieve are associated with the more negative aspects of ourselves. So many of the about 50 000 thoughts, which we have daily, are associated with the negative things that we discharge in the ether each day. So when we look at positive thoughts - positive thoughts with many people are so minimal, that many people are going through large areas of the day functioning in the negative states that they have often created themselves.

Working with exercises in this way can give you more understanding of how to use your thoughts in a productive way. Not just to create something that you can work with, or play around with, but in creating something that is constructive, to aid you in you getting a much deeper contact with yourself. Of course this requires courage.

If we had problems, emotional problems that have affected the bottom area of the body from the solar plexus downward, then those emotional problems have already prevented the natural flow of energy from getting through the bottom area of the body. So you have problems there, problems in expression, problems in sexuality, in emotional control. All of that comes about simply because the energy in the bottom area of the body is not sufficient to allow us to control and express from that area of the body.

———

I have been speaking about the differences of **polarity** between male and female. Those differences are important to know and understand, because so often we can become trapped in an astral state of consciousness. Becoming trapped in that, there is no real knowledge;

there is only the complete movement circulation that continuously goes on without moving beyond itself. So that when we come to real understanding of knowledge, that is situated in the growth of mind that of itself is related to the transpersonal point or individuality point above the head. Within that point we have the complete movement and fusion of energy that links up all of the chakras, and within that construction then many of the things that we relate to can give us the means of moving beyond the blockages or the difficulties that have trapped us into this astral state.

Discipline for many people represents what has happened at school, where the teacher said "you must do this", and if you didn't do it (at least when I was a child) he used to take a cane and smack you across the palms. Of course that is not discipline. What I am talking about as discipline is: to recognize within yourself the means of controlling what is going on from yourself in the way of emotion - for example: if you are continuously getting angry, try and understand why you are getting angry. Once having understood that then get some appreciation of how to **control** it.

That control then will of course come from a deeper area within you and that deeper area is situated in this point above the head (ID-point, DP). So discipline is not something that is holding you tight into an area, discipline is freedom, but we don't recognize it as that, because it is associated with something very harsh and cruel. Discipline is really freedom, freedom of expression that is not inhibited or limited by blockages that we have created ourselves. In this way, learning to appreciate that, for example, control of emotions is learning to understand that emotion itself is an outlet, which, if used correctly, releases energy just as sexuality can release energy. But if you use sexuality in an uncontrolled way, or if you use it in excess, as has been proven, then it can create states of schizophrenia. What I really mean is that discipline is not allowing the emotions or the instincts to run away without having some means of control.

The development process is very much related to control, as for example what we are doing now in this exercise. In having a problem relating your thoughts to breathing, that may be connected with something that happened to you, for example when you were a child, or what may have gone on in the birth process which of course makes it difficult to bring thought and breathing together. But if you have the means of working those problems out, that you do have, if you have the means of seeing that some emotions have been recurring with you many times through your life without you under-standing, then in doing exercises, bringing that forward, gives you an opportunity not only to look at it, but also to accept it and not reject it, and then do something about it. That in itself is a form of control or discipline. When things push you into activities over which you are not having control, such as emotions or fear that is a non discipline state, simply because you don't have understanding of yourself or a situation.

As you become more balanced in your physical action, then the storage of energy on the etheric shows itself to be more complete. In that, one has got to learn to express. **Expression** has two facets to it. One facet is a forcing, forcing oneself to do something. That is often very destructive, because so often we get ourselves into situations where we are forcing energy to move into a particular direction, in which it should not be moving. That comes about because of incorrect body activity associated with our thoughts, remembering that our thoughts are always the controlling area associated with body action or movement.

So, if we get ourselves into a forced situation of using energy incorrectly, then we are creating more and more stress between the astral state of consciousness and the physical body and that type of situation often ends up in problems. This is why we are always talking about emotional control. We always emphasize the necessity to understand your thought activity in association with other people. And this is so important, because often your projection onto other people is in reality a failure in yourself. When we speak about development, we are speaking about the development of ourselves, of learning to understand our own process as it relates to other people.

That brings us back to **expression**, because so many people close off when they get into a situation where someone disagrees with them, or they feel that someone doesn't like them, then immediately they close themselves off, no communication. All expression is vitally important in the whole process of learning more about yourself. The movement of energy in expression is very productive health wise.

Look at people who are introverted. Many people go through hell within themselves, simply, because they haven't got the means to open out, they have been trapped into an emotional situation, possibly when they were children, and so, as they go through life they are always covering up, never able to express as they need to express.

Your development process is to help you to appreciate you as an individual in relationship to other people, and the situations you encounter with other people, so that gradually you can learn to open out, so that your expression becomes more and more part of you as a real person.

When we build up energy in the etheric, then that energy must do something, so when we use exercises to change some energy structures in ourselves or around ourselves, then we must learn to express more and more of what we are building up, changes that are happening with us. What you bring in, you must also extend out!

Energy **blockage** is energy that is built up and is being held or trapped to some area of the body, some muscle or organ, so that eventually, the response in that muscle or that organ is not what it should be to the brain impulse. When this situation arises, then of course, the action of the body is not in accordance with what the thought processes want to happen. Then we get problems, pain. The actions of our physical body are so important to the whole process of energy function and movement. In all processes of development, the physical body is the last line of expression, a very important area of expression.

———

In the whole process there is never any let up, there is never any means of divorcing yourself from energy. You have always got to be working to keep contact with what you are trying to achieve or do with yourself. I have been working with people for nearly 30 years (1985), and it is still the same for me today as it was right in the beginning, I still have to spend a lot of time working with myself, a lot of time doing meditation. I had to learn to have patience, and the more you develop, the more difficult it becomes to have patience, because, if you develop the pineal you become more aware of activities than you were before. You can see movements of energy, so you can see what is needed with people, but of course to see what is needed and to have a person do it is a different thing. So, you have got to learn to have patience.

We have been working with healing now for quite a long time; Annie and I started healing in 1974. We have progressed healing, in that time from1974 to now, using natural energy flow, and so often we had to wait. Just now we are in a process of changing some of the things we are doing, and to make this change we had to wait for almost 18 months, because things were just not ready in the use of the whole energy. We had seen that 18 months ago; but it wasn't possible then to make the change, we had to wait until the whole cycle of activity was correct. Once you start to work with the whole aspect of using energy, then, as they say in English: patience is a virtue.

Transcriptions from courses of early 80's by Antje Martin

The things that are most important are what you feel with your heart not what you see with your eyes.

Spiritual Development

"One of the greatest difficulties in development is to get people to look at themselves."

"No matter what you have done in your life, it is there, it is yours, no matter what thoughts you have, they are there, and they are yours. You can't escape them, but you can work with them."

"Every part of your development relates to other people, not just to an introvert you. We have something that can bring us together to give healing to the world."

"Development is not a set of techniques: the reality of development is feeling, feeling for what you are doing"

"Development can never be a selfish structure"

Love

"How can you do something with love if you are rejecting yourself?"

"Your contact to love is the best protection you can have."

"You cannot force forgiveness. It comes when you are ready."

What are the permanent things in our lives as distinct from the impermanent things and these are all structures that are very much reflected in energy. In the many activities that we see functioning within energy, we very often find that some of these activities are moving in such diverse ways that often we have difficulty in being able to appreciate what they mean and what they are telling us. At times we all have to go through processes within ourselves which perhaps at the time are difficult, perhaps unkind even unnecessary. And yet, when we look back on it - if we accept the process, then we can realise we have learnt a lot.

....that is one of the first things that I remember from last year, after I had come through this problem with my heart. After a couple of days, I came around to more and more normal consciousness, and the thing that vibrated around me was the healing thoughts of many people. That was a tremendous upliftment, and it certainly brought to my conscious awareness the strength that can be created when many people use that level of their thinking or consciousness towards something which they would like to affect or help.

In these twenty years of being in Denmark, there have been many changes in the processes of understanding energy. And these changes are very significant because they also reflect changes that are taking place in the world that surrounds us. The increase of energy activity that has been noted over the past four to five years' is affecting many, many people in a way that presents opportunity to promote change.

Now, of course it is not everyone who recognises this increase of energy. It is not everyone who wishes to make changes within themselves related to what is taking place external to them. Many people, in fact, are held back, into the past of their own life structure and indeed have no wish or desire to move into the present.

And yet, the whole activity of life, in its reality, is demanding that we be in the present. This is something that seems to me to be increasingly important. That the changes that are going on around us, are not only affecting more and more people, but are causing increasingly difficult effects on the earth itself. The pollution that we create is, as many of us may know, reaching a state, that unless we make change, within the next ten years' we are going to be in dire straits.

The ozone layer which is part of the energy structure of the earth, created for our protection, we are helping to break it down. An increasing number of holes are appearing which allow the ultra violet of the sun to penetrate the surface of the earth. And this is increasingly happening. The effects that are being produced on the soil by our pollution, is creating, one can almost say, disaster. What has been produced over the past forty years has now moved upwards from where it had found its connection to the rock formation underneath the ground; and in moving upwards and producing an effect on the soil, we are getting much more toxins in the soil. ...

In speaking about this explosion on Jupiter (1994)... it is something that is taking place and of course when we come into such structures, trying to understand such structures, we do not have the answers as to why such things should take place. Anymore than we have the answers as to why there should be earthquakes. We know it relates to the stabilization of (tectonic) plates underneath the surface of the earth, but

Bob Moore – Feelings are the pathway to your soul

we still don't know why they should strike in the rhythm that they do strike in various countries or what that really means. Volcanoes and other structures of eruption have been taking place throughout time, and again we haven't the means to be able to appreciate why they take place, or the rhythm and the times that they take place.

There are some things that we can't know. Possibly because we have not evolved sufficiently to be able to appreciate what rhythm really is. As for ourselves as individuals, each one of us have various things that affect us. Some of these things perhaps we can understand, perhaps we can make change in, so that the effects that are created, which relate to a pattern, can be changed. There are some things that we can not change. Things which are part of what we have inherited, perhaps in the family background, which are contained in the gene structure of our makeup.

We have got to accept that these things take place. And perhaps this is one of the key words: Acceptance. Because we can not change everything, but if we can understand what progress is, then it becomes possible to accept. That acceptance is part of the structure that takes us beyond fear. Fear is one of the hidden activities which for many people, will often just strike, when they get into difficulties, whether that is physical difficulties, psychological difficulties, or difficulties between themselves and other people.

Fear is the activity predominantly related to the ego and many people try to avoid it, try to escape from it. In escaping from it, they are endeavouring to escape from themselves. This is where one can find people become very involved in judging other people. Judging other people, and often when one, in talking to such a person, gets into a depth of what it is all about, one finds that that person is running away from himself, trying to cover up his own fear, or something that they may be involved with within themselves. And so they place that on another person as a point of **projection**. We have many such things that are taking place around us at the present time. Manipulation is one of the predominant factors that one can see operating in how people live.

In all of this, our activity with ourselves becomes a very essential structure which of course will sometimes produce confrontations. Many times, such confrontations bring us to a point of not even recognizing ourselves, because we have tried to escape from that point so many times. All of this development is not an easy process. It is a process which for me is very important, and has been very important and still is extremely important. There is responsibility within it and that responsibility relates to all levels of oneself. Any true state of development is essentially progress, progress that relates to what you are doing in allowing yourself to open towards what you would consider to be a source, to a higher aspect of yourself. To be related to what you are seeking as under-standing through the learning process in this physical life.

In this, the relationship to energy is a relationship to many things. Energy is part of everything. And when we can obtain some acceptance of that, then it is possible, within this progress to have a more strong realistic connection to life.

Energy relates to all **belief**. Energy is part of the structure of all religion. Energy relates to creation. Creation, that they tell us about, where through the manufacturing of this 200 inch telescope in Switzerland, they claim that they have been able to move back to within 15 seconds of the creation of the universe. And that is moving back 150,000 million years. They have made some discoveries in this which are very important, I think, for everyone. ....

Those who have reached **stillness in meditation** will be aware that in reaching stillness you have moved beyond your own polarity. You have moved into an activity that is a growing activity, in which the only way that I could describe it, is that you are one with everything. Within deeper forms of meditation, there are possibilities to reach - as the theosophists or the Buddhists would tell us - the **seventh stage of consciousness**.

Certainly, there would seem to me, to be in that a very valuable structure to endeavour to reach. Most people would seem to be held into perhaps the fourth, maybe third, level of consciousness. The **fourth level of consciousness** consists of the structures that one can find in connection to energy that one would see in the health aura, or that reflect the thinking; particularly the 'busy mind' thinking that one can see in the mental aura structure.

Within all of this aspect of trying just to be aware that life, in its existence as we have come to know it now, has got something that we in the normal sense of reacting, can not find. We have got to move with our consciousness into another part of ourselves, which is a part that many people are not really aware of. Energy works on all levels. The energy that one sees with a person who is profoundly angry, one can also see with a person who is calm and not excited. The energy that one would see with someone who is fearful is the energy that one can find with a person who is compassionate.

Bob Moore – Feelings are the pathway to your soul

The difference being: how the person has developed or has learned to use themselves. Perhaps for many it is easier to allow oneself to be drawn in various directions. Indeed, one can find the reality is that there are not so many people who make true conscious decisions from themselves. Often decisions are coming from the insistence or the influence of other people.

So what does all this mean then, when we come to our own state of development? In what we have worked with in the years we have been together as a group, we have been endeavouring to bring your attention to different parts of yourself that show up in movements around your physical body and within yourself. Such movements show differently in various positions of your body. These movements that show differently, within the various positions, this is not new. And indeed, anything that we are teaching is not new. It has existed for thousands and thousands of years. But particularly in the West, we have suppressed the right hemisphere of the head. We have limited our own potential related to intuition, related to reaching levels of ourselves that operate beyond the physical, and we have placed more and more emphasis on education related to the left hemisphere of the head. There is nothing wrong with the education that relates to knowledge that we find in the analytical process of ourselves. But there are so many things that can not be understood from the analytical process that we use, relating to the left hemisphere of the head. There are many things in which we have got to move beyond the knowledge that we acquire through education. In going beyond that, the work with energy, is to endeavour to get a harmony, a blend, a balance, between the left and right hemispheres. None of us have the means, nor is it possible, to analyze intuition. All that we can do is analyze the effects of intuition and that brings us to what is functioning on the physical level.

If we are seeking to develop the awareness within ourselves that is showing with energy, we have got to take a step beyond the physical level, so as to incorporate the non-physical level with the physical. The insight that we gain as to the difference between what is **impermanent**, as to what is **permanent**, becomes a vital factor in what we are striving to reach within this deeper, awakening contact within ourselves.

In the processes that we use connected with energy, it is often going to bring forward experiences which many of you have had in this group, and perhaps in other areas of your life in working with energy, working with meditation. Experiences can be very valuable, but one has also got to recognize that experiences have got to be brought into your physical life. Not just used at a point of time, saying 'That was a wonderful experience'. Anything that is really wonderful helps you to live your life correctly.

Within this relationship that one finds in connection to energy, there are of course blockages, difficulties that we have created ourselves, which are held between the **etheric level**, as we call it, and the physical body. ...If you remember, the etheric level in reality is the subconscious level of mind. It is the storehouse. We can find different positions where energy is stored. And we remember that energy is a structure that helped to create you, as a physical body. The first eleven weeks after you were conceived, when you were being formed, the movement of energy proceeded every movement that was there related to the formation of your physical body. That indeed, is where we find some of the structures of hereditary factors playing a role, limiting the process of expression or limiting our means to do things because of family background, illnesses, or whatever.

Within all of this process, from the very point we were created, energy played its part. The sperm and ovum coming together, operated through **sound**, as medical science now tells us. Each individual sperm produced its own sound, the ovum producing its sound in the fallopian tube of the mother. The penetration of that one sperm into the ovum then began the whole process of **conception**. It would seem to me, in the studies I have tried to undertake in all of this, that preceding this connection between sperm and ovum, we must take into consideration the thought processes of the male and female, of the mother and father. What that produced, or gave the means to produce, in what was being created from that particular point of penetration of sperm into the ovum.

Our own thoughts are a vital factor in how we live. I mentioned a moment ago, that many people have great difficulties in making decisions. So often many people ask me what they can do to increase their abilities to see the aura structure. This is a question that keeps occurring over and over again. Well, the ability to see the aura structure relates to the use of your sensitivity and to how much you are prepared to go into using your self in a way that brings you into dedication. Dedication in what you are doing.

You know, if you just think back in your life - perhaps if you just think back one week in your life, and ask yourself 'How many **decisions** that I have made in this past week, have I really carried through? When you see the mental aura structure, one thing that is quite predominant in it is all the little black dots that one finds, particularly around the upper head, and even down into around the face. I discovered some years back that these little black dots were relating to decisions that people made that they never carried through.

Your thoughts are energy and if you produce a thought in wishing to do something, and before you have even started to do it, change that decision to something else, the energy is still there. You have not utilized the energy. It is still maintained in the position where your thought operated from.

Our lives are complicated, but often we have increased the complications because we have not paid enough attention to what development or growth really means. When we work with energy, we are not just working with your problems. I have tried to bring what I have said up to the moment, into what I consider to be a realistic structure in what is taking place. But the process of energy is not necessarily trapped into what many would consider to be a negative structure. There is a tremendous amount of joy that one can find in one's life, if one is prepared to look inside.

Each one of us has **light within us.** The light that we have within us is a light that one can see when a baby is born. And this relationship to energy at birth is one of the most important times of our lives. It has been one of the most enriching experiences that I have had, watching births and seeing energy in its movement with a number of mothers, this whole activity of the movement and the intensity of energy. If man could only learn, and inwardly digest, that before the physical body was created at all, energy existed.

When we die, **death** is an uplifting experience when one has the possibility to watch the whole movement of energy taking place. And perhaps this great debate as to whether a person is dead when their heart stops, or their minds stop working, would not exist as a debate, if people could only appreciate what the whole structure of energy is doing when a person is in a process, perhaps with a terminal illness.

The **silver cord** is talked about in the Bible. The person is physically dead when that silver cord, which I see as a type of shining mist, when that is broken. But until that is broken, the person is not dead, whether they are unconscious or not and the energy continues. The movement of energy reaches up, is attracted to the person's individuality point, and so circulates around that, and then disappears into another dimension. To learn as much as we can about such processes would seem to me to be an important contribution towards having more joy in living. To realize that we have come from somewhere and we are returning to somewhere. What takes place in between requires our attention, requires our increasing understanding of life.

Norwegian group 94, transcription G. Hatt

———

The process of personal development is essentially that of
learning about oneself, which involves the relationship to
energy within the physical body and energy external to
the physical body. One can find that the energy fields react
to the various circumstances in which one becomes involved
in one's life. As one would move beyond the curiosity stage,
which perhaps many are finding in their initial attraction to the
process of energy and personal development, one becomes
confronted with questions such as: Why would one wish to
pursue the whole art of development? What is my motivation
in wishing to develop? What am I going to use this increased
knowledge of energy for? How do I understand the purpose
of my life, through the increased awareness obtained within
development?

These questions are often confronting. To work with energy
within one's own structure of personal development is of itself
a serious business, because one is required to make decisions,
which often mean changes in one's life. It is necessary that
such changes take place, because one so often realises that
the things that one is doing are not helpful in progressing one's
life, or what one is reaching towards as a goal has become
too materialistic. As progress is made, various thoughts come
forward as to what change means and if indeed it is possible
to make changes in one's everyday activity. Development, in
relationship to understanding one's own life, is not going to be
accomplished within a few months or indeed a few years. It is
a progressive state, which one finds oneself involved with and
lasts for the remainder of one's physical existence. The various
processes that one becomes involved with in development
are often taking us away from such things as pride in
establishing something as superiority or indeed taking us away

from many of the emotions which have controlled our life structure. Emotions like anger perhaps or jealousy are things that hinder us from being able to appreciate a deeper relationship to ourselves and as a consequence sometimes mean that our connection to other people has become rather superficial. Being increasingly aware of the feeling connection to ourselves and the depths that one can experience, particularly in contact with the heart, brings us into a humbleness, in which we can appreciate a more real or true balance between ourselves and other people.

Within this process one often becomes aware of the need to express the feelings that we have about areas which are linked to the depth of our true nature. This is where one can find various aspects will show up with different people, realising that personal development is not something that is the same for each person. Its individual connection shows itself in the individual ways to register and to express outward. The attraction to the various structures that appeal to us to be expressed (like music, art, etc.) then become part of the whole process one finds within development through the use of energy.

Music which is essentially sound plays a very important role within all of this process. Music is the frequencies of various sounds that one finds in the different scales of music, which one finds both in the West and in the East. The use of music can indeed draw us deeper into ourselves in a very progressive way. My relationship to music is one which has helped me tremendously in the whole self or personal development process and has given me the opportunity to appreciate a more harmonious relationship to myself as well as a progressively harmonious connection to other people.

The relationship between energy in the energy fields and music is inseparable. One finds reactions within the energy fields to various sounds. Of course the search within many people is to find harmony, a greater peacefulness. Many types of music, from classical to so called 'new age' music can aid all of that process, which is a progressive process that is taking us from one level of understanding to another and thus aids the connection to meditation to provide for us means of reaching silence and stillness within ourselves.

One learns to listen to music as one learns to listen to oneself, not just with one's ears but with one's awareness. Not all music that helps us to progress is music that has a rhythm. Quite often music, which is described by many as sound rather than music, can have a penetrative effect. This provides the opportunity to release things that we would call blockages within ourselves, which limit our possibilities to perceive the connection to ourselves and indeed the connection to others more deeply. Music, I feel, is like development. One has the two aspects within it: the aspect of being able to analyse and understand the processes that take place within it - and this is part of the blend that exists between energy fields and music itself. On the other side one is also increasingly becoming aware of feelings, a word which immediately attracted my attention in the heading of this book: Music - the feeling way, a quest for harmony. This is basically as I would view it, the blend that one finds between music and energy. This is also an essential quality in relationship to healing and self healing.

From the foreword to 'Music – The Feeling Way'

"To understand yourself means working on yourself and working on yourself means going deeper, looking at different states of consciousness, the different degrees of contact that you have with yourself, and, above all, learning to love yourself."

"We must always remember that in anything that we are doing there has to be joy if it is to become real."

The Psykisk Center was founded to help promote the overall development and Growth of Individuals. The Center is not connected with any other Society, School or Institution, or associated with any Religious group or activity, but has adopted the following principles.

1. God as a Supreme Parent. Unchangeable , in Being, Wisdom, Power, Holiness, Justice , Goodness, Truth and Love.

2. Man as a Family. Truly United in Harmony, and purposefully motivated when Energized by Love.

3. Communion of Kindred Minds and Ministry of Evolved Souls.

4. Reality of living. Experienced in knowing, accepting and expressing Spiritual Qualities.

5. Spiritual Healing. The working of the Power of Love within the pattern of Natural Laws, channeled through Receptive Man.

6. Psychic Development. An inner process of Self Analysis, Self-Discipline and Meditation, allowing a gradual unfoldment and manifestation of Higher Senses.

7. Personal Responsabilité.

8. Compensation and Retribution for all right and wrong deeds.

About practicing the meditations and exercises:

You must be dedicated to it and give priority to it, or you won't gain from it but will leave yourself exposed to other people's thoughts and your own dense emotional states, which will keep you moving back to those states.

"Development is a consciousness of honesty"

An energy awareness exercise in Bob's style:

1) Take about 3-5 minutes to breathe with your awareness
    below your navel, into the lower belly area.
2) Next, draw a line on the skin surface down your right
    leg until you reach the sole of your right foot, stay there
    a while with your awareness. Then continue the line
    across to the sole of your left foot (through the air, so to
    speak), pause there, then move up your left leg until
    you reach your starting point again.
    You can do this for some 10-15 minutes

This exercise will help with your grounding and improve the
contact with your legs, feet and your hara area. It can be
very beneficial especially after having done a lot of 'head
work', such as working on a computer, studying, etc.

The main advice Bob would always give is to do any exercise
like this one, very slowly and with feeling. A more complete
explanation of the method of how to do such exercises is
explained in details in my book 'The Science of Spiritual
Healing.'

Index of Keywords

Sources of the texts

Page

Bob Moore   (1928-2008)

Bob Moore was born in Northern Ireland in 1928. After an education at a Quaker College he first studied to become a minister, but an interest in electricity prompted him to start a technical education in electrical engineering. He entered business life and became commercial manager in a supply and engineering company, a position he held until his move to Denmark.

He began teaching about energy in England. He then moved to Denmark in 1974 and founded, together with his Danish wife Anni, the 'Psykisk Center'. A variety of courses on meditation, colour and sound, energy awareness, healing and general self-development were offered. He taught in a number of different countries: Denmark, Norway, England, Canada, Brazil, Holland, Germany, Switzerland, to name some of them.

He developed a unique teaching including a major psycho-somatic part that led to one of the most detailed and integrated approaches to the physical body in linking it to thought structures, emotions, energy structures and to deeper aspects, through personal exploration and the help of self-discipline, exact structures (like triangles, squares, circulations) and, above all, one's feelings. He had an enormous understanding of the human energy fields (primary and secondary chakras, energy lines and their function). As he was seeing the aura he brought in a great precision together with a grounding of spirituality in everyday life.

Bob Moore – Feelings are the pathway to your soul

A. & A. Mauthner
'Conversations with Bob Moore'/'Samtaler med Bob Moore'

Books reflecting Bob Moore's teachings:

Daniel Perret
Music – The feeling way, free download (versions F, GB, D):
www.vallonperret.com / Danish version at Borgen
Roots of Musicality, Jessica Kingsley Publishers   (D, F, GB)
Sound Healing with the five Elements, Binkey Kok   (D, F, GB)
Science of Spiritual Healing, BOD   (D, F, GB)
Experience of Spirituality, BOD   (D, F, GB)

Helen Gamborg
'Das Wesentliche ist Unsichtbar'/'Det Usynlige I Helbredelse'

Jim Gilkeson
A Pilgrim in Your Body, Energy Healing and Spiritual Process
Energy Healing, a pathway to inner growth

2 Bob Moore websites:
www.moore-healing.info You will find a list of teachers there
www.vallonperret.com   Bob Moore